C0-ANZ-825

The Philosophy of Kant and Our Modern World

The Philosophy of Kant and Our Modern World

Four Lectures Delivered at Yale University Commemorating the 150th Anniversary of the Death of Immanuel Kant

EDITED BY CHARLES W. HENDEL

THE LIBERAL ARTS PRESS — NEW YORK

Published at 153 West 72nd Street, New York 23, N. Y.

Printed in the United States of America

PREFACE

Four lectures on "The Philosophy of Kant and Our Modern World" were presented at Yale University in March 1955 to commemorate the 150th anniversary of the death of Immanuel Kant. There was immediate witness to the significance of Kant in the sustained enthusiasm with which the lectures were supported by the university audience. This lively interest in Kant and appreciation of the lectures have induced the speakers to offer them to the public beyond the halls of Yale University.

The program issued for the lectures declared: "The four lectures are offered by members of the University who have been engaged in studying Kant in the conviction that his ideas and reasonings are of particular value for us in our present world. The series pretends, however, only to treat of the several aspects of this rich and important philosophy with which the lecturers have themselves been preoccupied." For publication the speakers have slightly revised their original texts and documented their quotations and references. In the hope of encouraging the reader to study further the several phases of Kant's philosophy in which he might be interested, they have supplied a short bibliography of recommended collateral readings.

Some reference to the published works of the speakers relative to Kant and to the theme of the lectures may be in order here.

John E. Smith of the Department of Philosophy has translated Richard Kroner's *Kants Weltanschauung* (Chicago: The University of Chicago Press, 1956) and has in preparation a translation of Kant's *Anthropologie.*

George Schrader of the Department of Philosophy is consulting member of the editorial board of *Kant-studien,* published at Cologne. His publications on Kant comprise: "The Thing in Itself in Kantian Philosophy," *Review of Metaphysics,* 2 (March, 1949), 30-44; "The Transcendental Ideality and Empirical Reality of Kant's Space and Time," *Review of Metaphysics,* 4 (June, 1951), 507-536; "Kant's Presumed Repudiation of the 'Moral Argument' in the 'Opus Postuum,'" *Philosophy,* 26 (July, 1951), 228-241; "The Status of Teleological Judgment in the Critical Philosophy," *Kant-studien,* 45 (1953-54), 36.

René Wellek, Professor of Comparative Literature, is the author of *Immanuel Kant in England, 1793-1838* (Princeton: Princeton University Press, 1931); "Emerson and German Philosophy," *New England Quarterly,* 16 (1943), 41-63; and a chapter on Kant and Schiller in *History of Modern Criticism,* Vol. I: *The Later Eighteenth Century* (New Haven: Yale University Press, 1955).

Charles W. Hendel of the Department of Philosophy has treated the philosophy of Kant in Chapters 2 and 14 of *Studies in the Philosophy of David Hume* (Princeton: Princeton University Press, 1925, shortly to be reissued by the Liberal Arts Press, New York); in "The Meaning of Obligation," in *Contemporary Idealism in America* (New York: The Macmillan

Company, 1932); in "The Status of Mind in Reality," *The Journal of Philosophy,* 31 (April 26, 1934), 225 ff.; and in an introduction to the translation of Ernst Cassirer's *Philosophy of Symbolic Forms,* Vol. I (New Haven: Yale University Press, 1953).

C. W. H.

CONTENTS

JOHN E. SMITH
The Question of Man, 3

GEORGE SCHRADER
The Philosophy of Existence, 27

RENÉ WELLEK
Aesthetics and Criticism, 65

CHARLES W. HENDEL
Freedom, Democracy, and Peace, 93

Selected Bibliography, 129

THE QUESTION OF MAN

John E. Smith

THE QUESTION OF MAN

By John E. Smith

I

IT IS SAFE TO SAY that man's intellectual concern has a way of swinging back and forth between two basic poles: man himself on the one hand, and what falls beyond him, whether God or the physical world, on the other. During certain periods the attention of thoughtful men has been directed beyond man either toward God as the ultimate ground of all things or toward the physical world as a vast system of things, powers, and relations. At other times man becomes *reflective,* in the special sense that his attention is turned in upon himself, while the outer world is allowed to fade into the background for a time and man's greatest concern becomes man himself. As a rule, a cosmological period, if we may use this expression to describe a time when interest in the physical world is dominant, is one in which man feels sufficiently sure of himself and of his standing in the world to risk a self-forgetful attitude. At such times man in his confidence dares to devote all of his ingenuity and his powers to the investigation and, as it may be, the control of the world surrounding him. In many ways Aristotle's thought is a classic illustration of the cosmological interest; throughout his writings there is revealed a passionate interest to know the natures and reasons of all things under the sun and beyond the stars, but it is a self-forgetful passion in the sense that it is not man himself who is the primary object of attention.

On the other hand, historical periods in which, as the couplet of Pope so neatly expresses it, "the proper study of mankind is man" are periods when man is forced in upon himself, when he is led to wonder and to ask who he is, why he is, and what the whole thing means. Socrates, of course, presents himself at once as the model of the thinker who asks about man and about his proper business in the world. There is that striking incident at the beginning of Plato's dialogue *Phaedrus,* when Socrates, called upon to explain the myth of Boreas and Orytheia, refuses, saying of all such explanations:

> I have no leisure for them at all; and the reason, my friend, is this: I am not yet able, as the Delphic inscription has it, to know myself; so it seems to me ridiculous, when I do not yet know that, to investigate irrelevant things.[1]

The question of man may, of course, arise in many ways and the precise meaning of the question will not always be the same, but in some form it is surely one of the perennial questions. It may present itself as the result of some significant scientific discovery in physical nature or about human nature; it may arise because of some widespread fear or sense of the vanity of life; it may follow in the wake of some tremendous catastrophe in social and political existence. Whatever the reasons for its appearance at a given

[1] *Phaedrus,* 229e-230a.

time, however, concern for the nature and destiny of man is not one which remains underground for any long period of time. For the historical character of human life and the complexity of the human animal demand that the question of man be raised ever anew and that the answer be not simply taken over from the past but developed with originality from the substance of contemporary experience.

Notwithstanding all our own current interest in the natural sciences and in controlling the physical environment, it is highly likely that Western civilization from the end of the seventeenth century to the present will be characterized by future historians and students of human thought as a time when the subject of man and his nature was never very far from the center of attention. It is clear that it is now a dominant topic. Not only have the historical catastrophes of the past decades driven us to ask whether man's most formidable enemy may not be man himself, but fears and anxieties of a more personal, psychological nature stemming, as they have, from the threat of individual anonymity in mass society, have had the effect of keeping attention focused upon our own nature and standing in the world.

Moreover, our experience in the modern world of power and power politics has led us to question whether knowledge of the physical environment and the technical control which often follows can be allowed to develop apart from all intelligible relation to the moral purposes and religious concerns of man. In other words, we have come up against the perennial problem of determining the ends and purposes which scientific knowledge should be made to serve. A recent writer in the (London) *Times Literary Supplement,* assessing the state of science in the modern world, has this to say:

> But although it is almost as obvious now as it was in Newton's day that the great ocean of truth still lies all undiscovered before us, the feeling of glad confidence has largely disappeared from scientific circles. In truth self-confidence has largely given way to self-questioning. . . . it is now generally recognized that the progress of science cannot be considered in isolation but must be related to man's ethical and spiritual standards.[2]

It would not be too much to say that man appears at the center of the three most pressing problems confronting Western civilization: (1) how to prevent the reduction of man to the status of a thing or object beside other objects in a mechanized world; (2) how to preserve a sense of individual moral and social responsibility at a time when skepticism and relativism control a great deal of ethical thinking; and (3) how to bring the steady advances in scientific knowledge within the scope and direction of moral and religious purposes. The peculiar character of all these problems is that they are made possible by the inner nature of the very being who must attempt to solve them. Hence from a purely practical point of view we should have no hesitation in agreeing with the French philosopher Malebranche

[2] *Times Literary Supplement,* August 24, 1951, p. iv.

when he declared in his *De la recherche de la vérité* (1674), "Of all human knowledge the knowledge of man is the most deserving of his study."

The age in which Kant lived, known to us as the Age of Enlightenment, was a period in which interest in human nature and in man's place in the universe began to assume a dominant importance. The previous century, described by Whitehead as the century of genius, achieved almost unbelievable success in the application of mathematics to the description of the physical world. This century bequeathed to its successor a picture of the world as a vast mechanical system moving according to laws discoverable and calculable, but it had left uncertain the relation between man and this cosmic machine. The century of Kant, unlike that of Newton and Leibniz, began to wonder whether man might be the one being who could not be interpreted merely as another part of the system. Kant was asking not only whether the being who possessed the knowledge that the world is a machine could be taken as belonging to it in the same sense as its other parts, but also what proper relation should hold between man's precise theoretical knowledge of the world and other aspects of his many-sided nature. Kant, consequently, sought not only to analyze the rational structure of mathematics, physics, and speculative metaphysics, but also to bring these disciplines into relation to man's moral, political, aesthetic, and religious life. He sought for purposes within the life of man and for man himself in the universe. The result of Kant's attempt is the view of reality as a system of reason which, precisely because it is imperfectly and incompletely known by man, imposes duties upon him and demands from him an inner worthiness of will which he can ignore only by sacrificing his rational nature and giving up all claim to being a member of the human species.

It does not matter that the period in which Kant lived and worked was considerably different from our own, nor is it even necessary that there be a high degree of similarity between them for us to be able to learn from Kant's answer to the question of man as it presented itself in his own situation. What is of moment is that we remain open and receptive to Kant in order to lay hold of ideas and insights which can contribute to the correct understanding and resolution of our own human predicament. The highest tribute that can be paid to any thinker is that those who come after him not only take him seriously enough to interpret their own lives by reference to him, but that they dare to believe that at least some of what he had to say is still true.

II

There can be no justification for any attempt to reduce Kant's philosophy to a single idea or confine it to any one subject matter. His thought is too complex and the variety of topics upon which he wrote clearly precludes any such simplification. Nevertheless, the main philosophical questions raised by Kant and the new method which he devised to treat them point back to human experience and to the structure of the "faculties" of man, as Kant liked to call them. Kant's transcendental or critical philosophy, involving what has come to be known as his "Copernican Revolution," [3] is a reflective approach to problems of philosophical significance. It does not start with a world of fixed objects, nor does it seek to analyze any aspect of reality directly and, as it were, naively. Kant's approach is, in a sense, *oblique,* in that it directs attention in the first instance to the activity of the rational subject and to the relation holding between the knowing, feeling, or acting self and the type of experience appropriate to these faculties. In the Introduction to the *Critique of Pure Reason* Kant explains the nature of transcendental philosophy as follows:

> I entitle *transcendental* all knowledge which is occupied not so much with objects as with the mode of our knowledge of objects in so far as this mode of knowledge is to be possible *a priori* (i.e., in so far as knowledge is dependent on reason and not derived from sense.) [4]

As the title of his first *Critique* makes clear, Kant marks out as his ultimate subject matter the structure and the limits of human reason, and in order to arrive at his conclusions he always starts with actual human experience and knowledge and then attempts

[3] See "Kant's So-called Copernican Revolution," in H. J. Paton, *In Defence of Reason* (1951), pp. 91 ff.

[4] A12, B25.

to discover the contribution made by reason to the forming and interpreting of that knowledge. What is unique in Kant's method is that it is not the *object* of knowledge or that of action which *first* engaged his attention, but rather the spectator or knower who has the knowledge or who must perform the act. In this sense it is correct to say that it is man and his reason which constitute the subject matter of Kant's philosophy. Those who describe his thought as "subjective" are right if they mean that Kant always analyzes the structure of man's faculties. But the so-called subjective drift of his thought must not be misconstrued, as it so often is, to mean that Kant is engaged in constructing a world out of materials wholly internal to the self. Kant, if we may state the point in paradoxical fashion, was of the opinion that man or the subject is not "subjective," but that subjectivity itself has an *objective* structure which is at the same time the structure of reason itself.[5] Careful attention to the great critical works of Kant shows that in every case his aim was the same: to analyze and disclose rational structure as it appears immanent in man's experience, whether in the domain of mathematics, physics, morality, or religion. One does no violence to the status of either God or the physical world in Kant if one points out that it is always through man and his experience that he approaches any subject matter. Nor is it an undue sim-

[5] It is interesting to note that Kant is frequently accused of subjectivism, in a derogatory sense of the term, by the same thinkers who also complain that he gave us a fixed table of categories which neither time nor process can change.

plification of critical philosophy to say that behind all the intricacies of Kant's thought stands man as the creature and bearer of reason. Man is, as it were, the point at which all aspects of the world are reflected. Hence when Kant makes reference to the hypothesis of Copernicus in astronomy as a parallel to his own experiment in metaphysics, he is simply calling attention in another way to the central position of man and reason. For just as Copernicus proposed to explain the movements of the planetary bodies by supposing that the spectator is in motion instead of being fixed, as ordinary experience would lead us to assume, Kant is proposing the thesis that knowledge must be explained by attending to the contribution which human reason makes to its formation. Once again it is man who is thrust into the center of the picture.

Having indicated the sense in which Kant's method itself brings man into the foreground of his thought, we may now consider his treatment of what I call "the question of man" in more detail. The ideas to be singled out as having the clearest and most direct bearing upon this theme are also intended to refer back to the current problems involving man and his nature which were mentioned at the outset. Their precise relevance to these problems must, unfortunately, remain more in implicit than in explicit form, since it will be impossible to return and show their application.

III

A well-known passage near the end of the *Critique of Pure Reason* runs as follows:

> All the interests of my reason, speculative as well as practical, combine in the three following questions:
>
> 1. What can I know?
> 2. What ought I to do?
> 3. What may I hope? [6]

These three questions are, upon reflection, seen to be the questions forming in turn the basis of the *Critique of Pure Reason, The Critique of Practical Reason,* and *Religion within the Limits of Reason Alone.* For our present purposes there might be little point in calling attention to these questions, were it not for the fact that in several other places in Kant's many writings he repeats them and adds a fourth question, the importance of which is evident at once. One such place is in the Introduction to his *Logic,* where Kant, after listing the questions again, adds a fourth, "What is man?" He goes on to comment on all the questions as follows:

> The first question is answered by *Metaphysics,* the second by *Morals,* the third by *Religion,* and the fourth by *Anthropology.* In reality, however, all these might be reckoned under anthropology, since the first three questions refer to the last.[7]

[6] A805, B833.

[7] *Kant's Introduction to Logic,* tr. T. K. Abbott (1900), p. 15; Hartenstein, VIII, 25; see also letter to Stäudlin (1793) in Cassirer, X, 205-207.

We may take Kant to mean that the proper replies to the first three questions will provide a comprehensive account of the nature and destiny of man. For in setting forth his view of the nature and limits of our knowledge, in making clear the manner in which we are to conduct ourselves in the world, and in seeking to show man's proper relation to God, Kant implicitly defines man, both in his powers and his limitations.

It is important that we avoid being misled here by Kant's reference to anthropology. It is true that he wrote and published a work bearing the title *Anthropologie,* a subject which, as Kant tells us in the preface, formed part of his academic lecture program "for some 30 years," [8] but this work does not actually provide us with any such complete doctrine of man as is suggested by the four questions previously cited. In fact, no single work of Kant's contains the answer to that fourth question, for nothing less than the critical philosophy as a whole is adequate to such a task. I shall make reference to the *Anthropology* in what follows, but just because so much of that writing is given over to what Kant himself in other places calls "empirical psychology," we cannot regard that treatise as containing his final word concerning the question of man.

In turning to the questions themselves, I shall lay the greatest stress upon the first two and touch only in passing upon the third question, the one dealing with the ultimate destiny of man. Kant's philosophy of religion is too complex and tangled an affair for

[8] Academy ed., VII, 122.

even a brief treatment and, moreover, it is certainly one of the least satisfactory parts of his thought. Kant, like most of his contemporaries, had little grasp of the religious dimension of human life over and above its moral implications. In this regard he was a true man of the Enlightenment. Even without paying particular attention to the third question, however, consideration of the other two will take us a long way toward the understanding of our main theme.

What can I know?

Man is, for Kant, above all a creature of reason: this much is clear and beyond dispute. But what Kant means by reason is what we next want to know. Reason for him is a complex affair, comprising within itself the *understanding* or the power, indeed the necessity, of thinking the content of experience by means of certain pure concepts or categories; *judgment* or the power to subsume particulars under general concepts; and *reason* in what we may call the proper sense of the term which is described by Kant as the drive or thrust of thought toward completeness and totality in cognitions. Reason in this sense, the sense uppermost in the often neglected third part of the first *Critique,* seeks for unity and completeness in thought going beyond anything to be met with either in ordinary experience or in science. Reason seeks to apprehend certain totalities which can never be given to us as objects of experience, but which nevertheless can and must be thought and which function as goals for the understanding. God and the world are, for example, just such totalities transcending sense experience which, according to Kant's view, it is the aim of reason to attain. These totalities or Ideas, as Kant calls them, are held up before us by reason and, could positive knowledge concerning them be attained, man would be able to complete the system of reason and satisfy his cognitive capacity within the purely theoretical sphere itself. But, unfortunately, this is precisely what in Kant's view man is unable to do.

Of all the views held by Kant, his doctrine of the limitations of human reason is perhaps the most familiar; everyone, or nearly everyone, knows that purely theoretical reason cannot prove the existence of God, and that the reason for this is bound up somehow with the difference between the idea of one hundred dollars and the circumstance of having one hundred real dollars in the hand. According to Kant's analysis of our faculty of cognition, knowledge in the strict sense is possible in a given domain of inquiry if and only if some form of intuition is also possible —sensible intuition in the case of physics and mechanics, and what Kant calls pure intuition in the case of mathematics. Since Kant denied to man any power of *intellectual* intuition, he could not but conclude that the sphere of pure reason directed toward the purely intelligible totalities such as God and the soul must fall beyond the border of knowledge proper. This view that pure reason, in its strictly theoretical employment, is unequal to the task of knowing the realities at which it aims is most frequently stressed as the main conclusion of Kant's thought. And indeed there would be no use in attempting to deny that this is so; Kant plainly and forcefully maintained that while mathematics and physics yield genuine theoretical knowledge, metaphysics, in the sense of a speculative knowledge of transcendent reality, does not and cannot yield anything of the kind.

Despite all this, however, there are two points to be borne in mind lest the conclusion become one-sided. First, Kant did recognize the reality of reason as a *power* distinct from understanding, or at least not reducible to understanding, and he regarded it as legitimately raising questions passing beyond the piecemeal questions of the natural sciences. Secondly, Kant refused to allow his strictures upon the competence of reason in its theoretical employment to result in the denial of all reality to the supersensible domain upon which it seeks to lay hold. These two points serve to call attention to the fact—a very important fact for Kant's conception of man—that Kant believed in reason and that he recognized as undeniable our human concern for completeness and totality in our experience. The fact that Kant denied man's ability to satisfy the demand of his reason in theoretical terms should not cause us to lose sight of the fact that he continued to believe in the presence and power of reason even in the theoretical sphere itself. The skepticism of Kant concerning human powers has certainly been overdone; Kant did not reduce reason to the proportion of the natural and historical disciplines, a fact which such little-read sections as the Discipline, the Canon, and the Architectonic of Pure

Reason clearly show. He never tired of stressing the inevitability with which the Ideas of reason arise, and he states time and again that although we cannot exactly do with them, we also cannot do without them. In a passage near the end of the *Critique of Pure Reason,* he says of metaphysics:

> We can therefore be sure that however cold or contemptuously critical may be the attitude of those who judge a science not by its nature but by its accidental effects, we shall always return to metaphysics as to a beloved one with whom we have had a quarrel. For here we are concerned with essential ends—ends with which metaphysics must ceaselessly occupy itself.[9]

Here man is suspended, as it were, between the actual and the ideal. He has genuine empirical knowledge of himself and the world around him, but he is unable to answer in cognitive terms the speculative questions to which his own reason drives him. And for Kant this was a genuine dilemma, made all the more difficult by the fact that the demands of metaphysics are not dependent upon subjective preferences and fancies, but are literally expressions of the nature of reason itself. "Human reason," said Kant in the very first sentence of the preface to the first edition of the *Critique of Pure Reason* (it is ironical, in view of the enormous difficulty of Kant's argument, that a conclusion of such importance should occur so early)—

> has this peculiar fate, that in one species of its knowledge (i.e., in metaphysics) it is burdened by

[9] A850, B878.

> questions which, as prescribed by the very nature of reason itself, it is not able to ignore, but which, as transcending all its powers, it is also not able to answer.[10]

Kant's way out of the dilemma in which man is thus placed is to replace the theoretical ideal of metaphysics as a complete system of cognitions, "sought," as he says, "solely in its character as a science,"[11] with the ideal of what he called the "whole vocation of man"—the bearing of all knowledge upon the interests, concerns, and ultimate destiny of man. Kant in this way sought to keep all learning and all science in touch with human purposes and ends. He has expressed very clearly in his *Anthropology* the human goal which is to replace the theoretical goal of metaphysics,

> All advances in culture through which man contributes to his education have as their goal the turning of this acquired knowledge and skill to some account in the world; and the most important object in the world to which such knowledge can be applied is man himself, since he is his own ultimate end.[12]

Regardless of the problems raised by this establishing of man as the final aim of knowledge, and they are many, the fact remains that for Kant knowledge remains forever incomplete and haphazard in character unless the various scientific disciplines are brought into some intelligible relation with each other and directed toward such ends as will serve to give them

[10] Avii.
[11] B866.
[12] Academy ed., VII, 119.

purpose for human well-being. "What *use,*" asked Kant in the Canon of Pure Reason, "can we make of our understanding, even in respect of experience (i.e., even in the theoretical domain), if we do not propose ends to ourselves?" [13]

What ought I to do?

The second question concerns man in the role of moral agent, and the line taken by Kant in its answer is dictated by the conclusion arrived at in the first *Critique*. Kant was puzzled, as were many of his contemporaries, about the proper place of man in the universe, particularly his relation to physical nature. It did not seem to him that man could simply be taken as one object beside others in the system of nature, for to do so would be to ignore at least two characteristics distinctive of man. First, as the possessor of reason, man shows himself capable of experience, or ordered representations, and of knowledge containing necessity in it. Both require for their attainment a display of *spontaneity* which is without counterpart in the known operation of physical systems. Secondly, man, as an active being pursuing his designs in the world, appears able to act in accordance with the *conception* of laws. In other words, at least some of the law-abiding conduct issuing from man is determined in its inner nature by the conception of the law informing it; it is this power of self-determination through reason which, in Kant's second *Critique,* appears as the concept of freedom.

[13] B844.

Above all, it is his capacity to act according to the conception of laws which makes it impossible for man to be wholly included within the system of natural laws.

Nature was conceived by Kant as the existence of things in so far as that existence is determined according to universal laws. Man, Kant holds, as a creature of nature is subject to these laws in so far as he *is* a creature of nature and nothing more. But on the basis of the fact of civilization and more particularly man's moral experience, also taken as a fact, Kant claims that man is something more than a being of nature; he is a being of freedom or a being in whose life reason can have a determining influence. In the *Anthropology,* Kant lays great stress upon a distinction between two approaches to the study of man, a *physiological* and a *pragmatic* approach. The first type has to do, he says, "with what nature makes of man," while the second concerns what man, "as a free agent, makes—or rather can and ought to make—of himself." And, as is well known, it is what man *ought* to make of himself which is decisive for Kant's view. As Cassirer expresses it, "Kant never takes the idea of the *homme naturel* in a purely scientific or historical sense, but rather ethically and teleologically. . . . Kant looks for constancy not in what man *is* but in what he *should be.*" [14]

In all the lengthy discussion about Kant's ethics in the past two centuries, the major share of attention has been given to the concept of freedom and its dialectic on the one hand and to the ultimacy of the

[14] Ernst Cassirer, *Rousseau, Kant, Goethe* (1945), p. 20.

sense of obligation on the other. Without suggesting here that these topics have been unjustifiably emphasized, I should like to direct attention instead to a neglected idea present in Kant's view of man as a moral being—the idea of man as capable of having a *character*. In making the distinction between what nature makes of man and what man makes of himself, Kant was resisting all attempts to reduce man to the status of a thing, even a highly complex thing, in the system of nature. The things or objects of the world of nature are just there; they behave in ways that can be discovered, described, calculated, and explained, and, while such behavior can even be regarded as following a rational pattern, it is a far different affair from the behavior of man. For, although man has a certain natural constitution and disposition given to him at the outset as a *being* within nature, Kant is more interested in the moral quality which man can reveal through the manner in which he *acts* in the world. Man is called to make something of himself in the moral sense and, for Kant, this always has reference to the quality of *will* a man exhibits. In discussing the nature of the human species in his *Anthropology,* he says: "The primary characteristic of the human species is the power as rational beings to acquire a character as such." [15] And by a character Kant meant that peculiar "property of the will according to which the subject binds himself to definite practical principles which he has unalterably prescribed through his own reason." [16]

[15] Academy ed., VII, 329.
[16] *Ibid.,* VII, 292.

The possibility of having moral character, or of making oneself into a being bound by principles, is, for Kant, an achievement which elevates man above the level of physical nature. For to be a thing of nature is simply to be determined by laws, but to be a moral being is to be an *agent,* to succeed in determining the will through reason in a situation where it is possible to fail. Indeed, it is just because a character is not something *given* by "nature" but something which must be achieved in the sphere of freedom that Kant assigned it a place of such importance in reality. The moral quality of the self, he never tires of repeating, is what alone has *worth* in the world, and the measure of its value can be seen from the fact that it has no measure; character is absolutely good and has no value in exchange.

What most needs to be borne in mind in discussing Kant's view of the moral nature of man is that it is all based upon an initial conviction concerning the nature and status of reason in the world. Kant, I must repeat, believed in reason and especially in its power in action. It is in the sphere of moral action and in that sphere alone that reason, to use his own terminology, becomes *constitutive* and passes beyond its merely regulative function. Man is thus the particular channel through which reason is able to realize itself as it essentially is.

IV

After having considered briefly the question of man through the questions Kant himself singled out, we may still ask whether there is not to be found some single idea or doctrine which expresses or sums up more neatly than any other Kant's view of the nature of man. I believe there is such an idea and that it is the idea of man as *active* or *living* reason. Man, in his essential nature, is, for Kant, an agent, *the* agent in fact, apart from God. What this means is that, through freedom, man's task is to *will* the internal connection between his own individual reason and the moral law, or that reason which is universal for all men. In interpreting the meaning of Enlightenment in his little paper of 1784, "What is Enlightenment?" Kant proposed as the motto of that movement, "Have courage, dare to use your own reason!"

Kant was not, of course, the first philosopher to characterize man as a rational being. Many thinkers, in the name of different conceptions of reason, had done that before him. But what is new in Kant is his idea that rationality is an *achievement,* something which requires resolution and action. Reason is not a fixed property for Kant, but a power which human will must exercise. Whereas the things of the world exist within certain fixed limits, man is the being of freedom, and this means that he cannot show himself as a creature of reason unless he actively determines himself in a manner which accords with reason. Moreover, in the theoretical sphere as well, man must labor in order to achieve knowledge; and although the satisfaction of reason is not to be found in theoretical knowledge, even in that sphere the quest for more and more unity in knowledge and for the discovery of the relation between knowledge and man's purposes remains as a *task* to which man must address himself without end. Thus in Kant both knowing and proposing the ends to which knowledge is to be put are *obligations.*

More important than knowing, however, is the primacy of the act where man's moral nature is in question. The primacy of the practical in Kant means, as Cassirer used to say, interpreting Kant and paraphrasing Fichte, the priority of the *act* over the *fact.* So important is the act for Kant that he is not even satisfied with the man who *believes* that honesty, for example, is the best policy; in Kant's view, actual honesty, willing truthfulness and acting honestly, is better than any policy.

In concluding, we can do no better than to allow Kant to speak for himself concerning man and the value of the critical philosophy for his life:

> If there is any science man really needs, it is the one I teach, of how to occupy properly that place in creation that is assigned to man, and how to learn from it what one must be in order to be a man. Granted that he may have become acquainted with deceptive allurements above him or below him, which have unconsciously enticed him away from his distinctive station, then this teaching will lead him back again to the human level, and however small or deficient he may regard himself, he will suit his assigned station, because he will be just what he should be.[17]

[17] Hartenstein, VIII, 624 ff.

THE PHILOSOPHY OF EXISTENCE

George Schrader

THE PHILOSOPHY OF EXISTENCE

By George Schrader

A RECENT VISITOR to our University, a philosopher, presented a lengthy and somewhat tedious analysis of the meaning of two common one-syllable English words. The speaker was evidently intelligent and learned, sometimes witty and always clever. Upon being questioned why he, as a philosopher, was engaged in such pursuits, he replied: "This is just the way I like to potter around." If his words are taken at face value he seems to be admitting quite candidly that what he is doing has no great intrinsic importance. And he seems to imply, further, that he is aware of no work of great importance which he, as a philosopher, ought to be doing or even might be doing. Not only is he just "pottering around" but, presumably, that is all there is for the philosopher to do—and happy is the man who has found something that may occupy him!

But surely, you might say, we must not be so naïve as to take the man at his word. He is simply being modest, refusing to make pretentious claims for his intellectual pursuits! Has he not revealed the naïveté of the question in the sophistication of his answer? The questioner discloses an immediate concern, the desire to relate all inquiry to his own personal situation. The speaker, on the other hand, is beyond immediacy, detached, unconcerned. He looks at what he does with wry amusement, asking of it no momentous results. He sees the unimportance of what he does and therein the unimportance of all human activity. As an enlightened and detached thinker all things are to him transparent. He sees through the question as, also, through the questioner.

Such enlightenment and poise would appear to be the mark of confidence and security. If all questions are not answered, at least one knows how to take them. Is this not the manifestation of true orientation in thought, to be able to dispose of all questions without perturbation? The philosophically sophisticated man, like his socially sophisticated brother, is never to be taken by surprise. His wit and his cleverness can rise to any occasion. He can talk equally well about everything, for there is nothing really baffling or mysterious. All is transparent. Man cannot hope to master everything in his knowledge, but he can hope to see through everything to recognize that it has no meaning which escapes him. Is this not the goal at which the educated man should aim—the mastery of the world through insight?

We must be careful in our answer not to be Philistine, or to take too dim a view of pottering. Perhaps we need, along with Stevenson's "Apology for Idlers," an "Apology for Potterers," since most of us potter and would staunchly defend our rights. Pottering is a valuable antidote to fanaticism, a counterbalance to enthusiasm. But the question is not really whether we are justified in pottering or even whether we should potter, but whether there is anything more to be done than pottering. Granted that there are trivialities and banalities, idle talk and meaningless chatter, is all that we say so empty, all existence so transparent? Is the transparency really the fundamental characteristic of our world and ourselves, or only a seeming? Do we see everything as surface because there is nothing substantial, or is it but the reflection of our own insubstantiality which blinds us to the presence of mystery? Is even language transparent, and is reality transparently revealed in language? Is our sophistication a mark of security or a testimony of despair? Have we found an orientation for our existence, or only surrendered all hope of finding one? Do we wander about hither and yon because we are world-weary or because we are in fact lost?

I have made reference to the problem of pottering for two reasons: first, because it serves well to distinguish what might be called the existential from an avowedly nonexistential orientation in philosophy, and, secondly, because it raises the fundamental question of what it means to be oriented in one's thought. Does orientation imply detachment and indifference, or involvement and passionate concern? Is philosophical truth something to be dabbled with, or a matter of critical importance? Does it lie on the surface, to be skimmed from our commonest utterances, or is it deeply hidden, to be reached only by the most prodigious effort? The problem of orientation is a perennial one which lies at the center of all philosophical inquiry. One might even say that it is the most basic of all problems, though this would be to misrepresent it. For it is not a problem alongside other specific philosophical questions, but rather is thematically expressed in all philosophical questioning. Above all else the philosopher is seeking to orient himself, to find a place whereon to stand in employing the leverage of his reason. With firm ground under his feet and a focus for his imagination he can probe the deepest of mysteries. Without orientation he can only flit from point to point, making no sense of anything.

Philosophy is born of wonder. To be capable of questioning philosophically one must be capable of being lost in the world or, more accurately, of recognizing that one is lost in the world. The philosopher —and here I speak of no professional class—is forever lost and trying to find himself. When he is no longer inquiring about himself and his place in the world, his problems cease to be philosophical and become technical. It is the perennial necessity of questioning his orientation which makes philosophical inquiry dialectical.

To the best of my knowledge, Immanuel Kant is the only philosopher who ever wrote an essay on the explicit theme of orientation. In 1786 he published an essay under the title: *What Does It Mean to Orient Oneself in Thinking?* [1] He was concerned especially with metaphysical knowledge, but began with a consideration of geographical orientation. What he says on this point is so ordinary that at first sight it hardly appears worthy of a thinker of such distinction. It is really very simple to orient oneself geographically, he says, for I can always appeal to the fact that I have a right and a left hand. "Without the

[1] Cassirer, IV, 349 ff.

capacity to distinguish between motion from left to right and that in the opposite direction . . . I would be unable to determine a priori any difference in the position of objects. . . ." "Thus I orient myself geographically by all the objective data of the sky only by virtue of a subjective ground of distinction [namely the right or the left hand]. . . ." [2] This is a perfectly simple observation, but not so ordinary as it appears, for it lies at the base of Kant's theory of space and time, and thus of his theory of knowledge. One of the reasons which Kant gives for holding that space is intuited is the impossibility of perfectly interchanging a right-hand for a left-hand glove.[3] Conceptually they are the same, but the difference obtrudes itself upon anyone who has ever attempted to interchange them—or to put a left shoe on a right foot. The important point here is that, in Kant's view, in our intuition and construction of space, which provides the frame for all human experience, we begin with our own body. We orient ourselves "only by virtue of a subjective ground of distinction." However elaborate and comprehensive our conception of space and the world in space may be, it is always tied to the simple fact of our having a right and a left hand. Kant was a stubborn empiricist who believed that the starting point in knowledge is always the finite and particular individual. It would obvi-

[2] From "What Is Orientation in Thinking?" in *Critique of Practical Reason and Other Writings in Moral Philosophy,* tr. L. W. Beck (1949), p. 295.

[3] Cf. *Prolegomena zu einer jeden künftigen Metaphysik,* § 13, Cassirer, IV, 34 ff.; see also *Von dem ersten Grunde des Unterschiedes der Gegenden im Raume,* Cassirer, II, 395.

ously provide little solace to a man lost in a forest to know that if he stands still he can be quite sure of what is to the right and what is to the left of him. Yet a map of the region is of little use unless he knows what actually is to the right and what is to the left. It is necessary to establish a connection between the map and the situation of one's own body before one can make an intelligent move.

The significance of this point for orientation in thought is even more apparent when we consider it in relation to the "Copernican revolution" which Kant introduced into philosophy. Instead of attempting to begin with the certainty of God's existence, or with absolute being, we must begin with our own existence. All attempted demonstrations of the existence of God rest ultimately, Kant believed, upon the ontological argument. They take a transcendent objective ground as the starting point and attempt to account for man and the world. But this is essentially a speculative endeavor, Kant argued. To reach God we must move beyond the familiar world of experience. And for this we require a principle which will guarantee that we are not simply deluding ourselves. In this respect Kant is fundamentally a Cartesian, though more consistent than was Descartes. Descartes appealed to the certainty of God to warrant self-certainty, but he also appealed to self-certainty to demonstrate the reality of God. Kant made a firm decision on this point which is consistent with his general conviction about orientation—namely, that man has no alternative but to begin with his own existence. The proofs of the existence of God, like the certification of objects in space, must have a subjective ground. In our knowledge, whether scientific or metaphysical, we must begin where we are, with our own existence. This shift in orientation from transcendent reality to the finite subject constituted an essential moment in the "Copernican revolution." It gave rise to a reassessment of truth and a new interpretation of knowledge.

Kant did not effect the "Copernican revolution" singlehanded. Descartes and Hume had prepared the ground, and the rise of modern experimental science had made it inevitable. Classical philosophy from Plato to Descartes had been theologically oriented. The divine reason served as the model for human thought and the divine power as the warrant for human knowledge. Descartes saw clearly that classical thought rested upon a fundamental and unquestioned faith. Forced to skepticism and disbelief, he attempted to shore up the structure with rational demonstrations. But his formulation of the ontological argument is altogether unconvincing, for it presupposes the faith which it is attempting to supplant. Descartes recognized the necessity for providing a foundation for classical metaphysics, but he failed to see that it could not be done by transforming faith into rational belief. The disintegration of classical philosophy was a necessary precondition for the emergence of a new epoch. It entailed a loss of faith, but also a much clearer understanding of the nature of faith.

Descartes has often been referred to as the "father of modern philosophy," and not without justification. He was actually a figure of transition who exhibited as much allegiance to the old as savor for the new. But in his skepticism and his subjectivism he inaugurated the new era in which we yet remain.

Whereas Descartes was an unhappy figure who found himself forced to question the faith which had nurtured him, Hume approached the new predicament with enthusiasm. Almost gleefully he saw the old foundations crumble and heralded the transformation of knowledge into subjectively grounded belief. We are all nostalgic at times, and in our nostalgic moments we are inclined to regard Descartes and Hume as having robbed us of our heritage, of having introduced an era of subjectivism which deprives us of the certainty and confidence of our classical forebears. And those who have little taste for revolution consider the emergence of subjectivism an unqualified loss. Like the faithful remnant of the royalist party, they devote themselves to the work of counter-revolution, attempting to return to the grandeur of an earlier day. But the Bourbons are gone, and even the most steadfast pretender knows that Versailles cannot be returned to its former glory. Like all nostalgia, this one is based upon an illusion. To replace the monarchy would not be to recover the substance which made it possible. If we are to have a metaphysics or a social order which is not founded on self-deception, it must be developed from a soil which is our own.

Kant did not inaugurate the revolution but he consolidated it, turned it from a mere destructive force to a formidable constructive power. If metaphysics cannot be founded upon the ontological argument, then it must find a new center. The "I doubt" of Descartes, which seemed to provide the fatal challenge to any metaphysics, Kant undertook to transform into the basis for metaphysical inquiry. In subjectivity Kant saw more than an embarrassment. He found there the sole possibility for the justification of human knowledge. One of Kant's greatest contributions to philosophy was his disclosure that knowledge is a mode of subjectivity. Hence to level the charge of subjectivism against this theory of knowledge is to misunderstand it altogether. It is a large step from Kant's thesis that knowledge is intrinsically subjective to Kierkegaard's contention that truth is subjectivity, but there can be little doubt that Kierkegaard's claim is predicated on a Kantian foundation. Curiously enough, Hegel and Kierkegaard are in agreement in the form of the assertion. They differ in that for Hegel the subject is potentially absolute, whereas for Kierkegaard it is irrevocably finite. These two monumental thinkers provide us with alternative variations on a fundamental Kantian theme and thus enable us to see more clearly what is involved in Kant's position than would otherwise have been possible.

Knowledge, as Kant analyzed it, is the mode of our apprehension of reality. To know is necessarily, however, to apprehend mediately and indirectly. Intuition which lays claim to immediacy remains forever blind unless informed by the categories of thought. To know is to grasp reality in objective form, to objectify it. Knowledge is grounded in a universal human need, the need to orient oneself in the world. If we were only animal we would have no need for knowledge, for we would always be immediately oriented. Since we are beyond the level of immediacy, the only way in which we can orient ourselves is through thought. But since thought is ever dependent upon immediate intuition for its content, it is limited to representation (*Vorstellen*).

Science, like common sense, is the representation of reality to the human subject in objective form. Thus on the one hand science serves to relate man to reality through the mediation of appearance. But at the same time it erects an increasingly formidable barrier between man and reality. Now if, as Kant held, knowledge is intrinsically a mediate relation to reality, the progression in scientific knowledge is in inverse relation to the attainment of reality in itself. In other words, knowledge constitutes an overlayer on the thing-in-itself. In the development of our knowledge we do not strip away the appearance to behold the thing in its pristine character, but pile layer upon layer of phenomenological construction. If Kant's contention appears perverse, think for a moment of attempting to grasp the inner being of so simple an object as a rock while entertaining all that science has to say about it. Our conception of the rock objectifies it, represents it to us in thought so that we can relate ourselves to it and use it with considerable success. But it does not and cannot pretend to give us the integral being of the rock.

Knowledge, then, is subjective on Kant's analysis precisely because it is objective. We are, he maintained, capable of an indefinite progression in our cognition of the world, but we proceed always on a horizontal plane. We cannot make the vertical movement to reality in itself even by an infinite horizontal movement within experience. Immediacy is lost at the beginning and is not to be recovered by the further elaboration of the mediation. This is the necessary and inevitable limitation of human reason in so far as it is engaged in cognitive inquiry. The possibility of human knowledge presupposes the alienation of man from himself and the world, and the development of knowledge only accentuates the alienation.

When stated so baldly, Kant's theory seems to offer only the most dismal view of man's efforts to apprehend reality through knowledge. It puts serious strictures not only on our gross knowledge but on the most refined scientific cognition. Yet as a theory of knowledge it has been widely embraced by scientists since Kant's time. It is not that the scientist undervalues his own work, but rather that he views it as an infinitely perfectible human task, the goal of which is not to achieve immediate unity with transcendent reality, but to appropriate it for human ends. Of course, he is not a crass utilitarian expecting always to win concrete benefits from his work, but in the larger sense he sees his investigations as "practical" and pragmatic. He knows that without a method he is lost and, as Kant put it, he "cannot go to nature empty-handed" but only with questions which he stubbornly insists upon having answered. He is an empiricist, but also an experimentalist who always retains the control over the data with which he works.

His theory is infused with imagination, his constructions with genius. He finds himself in the world only because he projects himself into it. Yet his product is not the creation of sheer fantasy, for it is anchored always in the immediacy of fact. It is this connection between data and construction which makes it science rather than mere conjecture. But it is the scientist who holds the two together, and in his awareness of this the scientist has no doubt of his own importance. In the unity of his own person, the scientist holds together the abstract and the concrete, the universal and the particular. He furnishes in his own existence the necessary subjective ground for his inquiry.

Since Kant's day there have been many variations in the interpretation of this doctrine, and some vigorous attempts to repudiate it. But in general it has constituted a major theme for subsequent explorations and provided a frame for inquiry. In the variations which have been offered one can discern two extreme and opposed developments, the absolutist and the existential. Hegel saw at once the force and power of Kant's analysis. Persuaded that knowledge is mediate and subjective, he attempted to eliminate immediacy through absolute mediation. Dialectic is the process of mediating between substance and subject, finite and particular, appearance and reality. Subjectivity is inherently self-transcending, so Hegel thought, and is capable of overcoming the alienation between subject and object by a process of infinite self-expansion. But it is important to note that Hegel did not attempt to go beyond Kant at the level of understanding or even of speculative reason. To overcome the alienation between the self and its object Hegel marshaled all the powers of spirit. It is absolute spirit, the creative source of culture and history, which achieves the ultimate reconciliation. Art, morality, and religion are required to supplement the work of cognition in closing the circle which encompasses man. For Hegel the truth is the whole, the total process of mediation which mediates itself.

At the other extreme from Hegel lies the revolt of Kierkegaard against the infinitizing of the human subject. Whereas Hegel had taken the phenomenal object as a middle term and exploited it to bring the whole of reality within experience, Kierkegaard reinstated the duality between subject and object in the most radical fashion. In effect he eliminated the phenomenal world altogether and left man without the promise of mediation. God is absolutely transcendent and wholly other. Man is pure subject to himself. What Kant had taken more or less for granted as the subjective ground of knowledge, Kierkegaard regarded as a supreme task. The self is not given as a reality either phenomenally or noumenally, but as a possibility. Man's chief problem is to become an authentic self. Heidegger, Jaspers, and Sartre follow Kierkegaard in stressing the problematic character of human existence, and the absolute imperative of achieving authentic self-existence.

But it is unfair to consider the relation of Kant either to Hegel or Kierkegaard without taking into account Kant's treatment of the practical reason. Both Hegel and the existentialist philosophers are as much indebted to the practical side of Kant's philosophy as to his analysis of cognition. From the standpoint of speculative reason, Kant had maintained, it is impossible for the self to know itself as it is in itself. It can only view itself as an object or representation. In cognition the self is essentially a spectator to itself and the world. But from the standpoint of morality with its demand for action the matter is altogether different. Here the self is disclosed as a subject for itself confronted with the task of realizing itself through the exercise of will. The self is free, but it must affirm and realize its freedom in the form of autonomy. It is a subject, but must achieve the actualization of its subjective being.

Kant rejected all naturalistic accounts of the self, insisting that it has no given nature or essence which as a potentiality only waits to be realized. It is impossible, Kant maintained, to derive an ethics from an analysis of the nature of man.[4] There is no natural law governing the realization of selfhood, but only the conception of law.[5] The imperative of morality is not a law but the principle of law. In the exercise of his freedom and the expression of his will man must give himself a law, must provide a structure for his existence. Autonomy and self-existence are not given potentialities but possibilities. The possibility itself is transcendent and indeterminate. In his interpretation of principles and ideals Kant is clearly more of a Platonist than an Aristotelian. In fact, he expressly

[4] Cf. *Grundlegung zur Metaphysik der Sitten,* Cassirer, IV, 267 ff.

[5] *Ibid.,* pp. 257, 258.

acknowledges his indebtedness to Plato in the interpretation he gives to ideals.[6] But Kant differs from Plato in two respects: (1) he grounds the ideal possibility in the human will, and (2) he interprets it as a dynamic principle rather than a static form.

From the standpoint of morality man is primarily a will, and a will is a power of spontaneity.[7] The fundamental characteristic of man as a moral being is his freedom, and since freedom is a power, it has and can have no *essential* form. We can never examine freedom in any of its expressions or manifestations in such a way as to determine its nature, for it is precisely the character of freedom to be capable of transcending any of its modes of expression. In viewing it otherwise we would inevitably regard freedom as a potentiality and the expression as its natural form. We can see Kant's point with special clarity when we consider his analysis of the process of artistic creation. Beauty, he maintained, is both an ideal and a principle. We can examine those works of art which represent the creative activity of the artist, but we can never discover the essence of beauty or even the form of beauty in the world of art. At best we can make empirical generalizations to the effect that the artist tends to create certain types or kinds of work.[8] But as soon as we attempt to go beyond this sort of criticism we are guilty of confusing the form of the work of art with the principle employed by the artist in creating it. And so it is also with morality. We

[6] *Critique of Pure Reason,* A570, B598.
[7] *Kritik der praktischen Vernunft,* Cassirer, V, 62.
[8] *Kritik der Urteilskraft,* Cassirer, V, 284.

may examine the lives of good men, but we can never discover in this manner any natural form or essence either of man or of a good man. We can say only that some men have exercised their freedom in such a way as to produce a life of this sort. To attempt to imitate either the artist or the morally good man would be the sheerest folly, for we would be attempting to effect by mechanical devices what he produced through the exercise of freedom and genius.[9] Examples in art and morality, as also in science, are useful, for they may suggest to us the possibilities of creative expression. We may see what a man can be, what he is capable of creating. This may awaken us to the possibilities of freedom in ourselves. We may, indeed, undertake to express our own freedom through the imitation of others in the same way in which a child learns to use language. But it is our own form and character that we must develop, and imitation is at best a crutch to aid us in grasping the principle itself.

No man, in Kant's view, is born with a moral character. He is endowed at birth with neither the actuality nor the potentiality of one. If he is to have a character at all, he must create it. It is a possibility which confronts him, but again not as anything determinate. He has no model to guide him, but must construct it. The model is the form in which he represents himself to himself under the idea of freedom. If he takes the model too seriously, he negates the

[9] "Imitation has no place in moral matters, and examples serve only for encouragement." *Critique of Practical Reason*, tr. L. W. Beck, *op. cit.*, p. 68.

freedom which it was intended to serve and instruct. To use Kant's terminology, the model is a schema and functions symbolically. It gives expression to the ideal in concrete form and thus provides a rule for action; but at the same time it refers beyond itself as does the work of art. A morally good life, like a work of art, must be taken as the symbolic expression of freedom.[10]

Freedom for Kant is radical but not absolute. The expression of freedom depends upon reason which limits and restricts it. As Kant interprets it, reason in its practical employment plays a double role. On the one hand, it is instrumental to the exercise of will and the realization of subjective existence. But, on the other hand, it transcends the will and provides a principle for its autonomous expression. Kant found it difficult to express this twofold character of the function of reason. He stressed one or the other aspect at different times, but more frequently the transcendent function. But both functions are essential, for Kant means to establish that through reason the will transcends itself. Quite apart from the intrinsic difficulty of finding adequate means of expressing this truth, Kant did not have available the necessary conceptual tools. He insisted upon the practical role of reason, the fact that it is grounded in the will, though providing a law for the will, even at the risk of falling into apparent contradiction.

The similarities between Kant's view of man and the views of contemporary existentialist philosophers

[10] Cf. *Kritik der Urteilskraft,* § 59: "Von der Schönheit als Symbol der Sittlichkeit," Cassirer, V, 428 ff.

are not difficult to grasp. Kierkegaard, Heidegger, Jaspers, and Sartre share Kant's conviction that the self is fundamentally a possibility for existence which can realize itself only through freedom. Sartre borrows certain basic categories from Hegel in his own analysis of self-existence, but he is Kantian in his insistence upon the radical character of freedom. Hegel, too, accepted much of the Kantian position and attempted to provide a more exact and more complete account of the way in which self-existence is achieved. His analysis of the relation of substance and subject, of the in-itself, the for-another, and the being-in-and-for-itself provide useful conceptual tools for articulating Kant's doctrines. Nevertheless, Hegel subverted the Kantian position by treating possibility as potentiality and thus naturalizing human freedom. Hegel's great insight, which is of decisive importance for Kierkegaard and the existential tradition in philosophy, was to recognize that through action and the exercise of freedom the self becomes objective and alien to itself. Thus we find in Kierkegaard and the existential philosophers the examination of authentic and unauthentic modes of self-existence. This theme, which is so fundamental to existential philosophy, could never have been derived from Kant alone. It represents the combination of the Kantian doctrine of freedom with the Hegelian concept of alienation.

To those who are familiar with Kant's writings this may sound very strange, for, one might object, did Kant not have a carefully formulated distinction between the noumenal and the phenomenal self? Indeed, Kant made such a distinction, but he did not interpret it in the manner of Hegel and Kierkegaard. For Kant the moral world and the world of objective empirical existence are so sharply separated that he could see no dialectical relation between them. He believed that the phenomenal is the expression of the noumenal, but he supplied us with no categories for examining the relation between them. How the noumenal gives rise to phenomenal processes remains a complete mystery in Kant. We are told that it is through the spontaneity of freedom that this occurs, but the role of freedom as it emerges from the one realm into the other is never systematically analyzed. As Hegel interpreted the relation between the two, the objective world is the necessary expression of freedom but, at the same time, the negation of it. To act, Hegel says, is inevitably to be guilty. Kant had seen clearly that to *know* oneself is to objectify oneself but not so clearly that to *will* and to *act* is to *transform oneself into an object.*

For Kant the fundamental conflict in which man is involved is rooted in the depth of his will. He must choose whether his reason is to be subservient to his natural desires and inclinations or to be legislative and prescriptive for his natural existence. The will is divided within itself and against itself. The self-alienation expressed in the moral situation is the original division of the will within itself.[11] As in the case of cognition, the will has moved beyond immediacy in

[11] "For the will stands, as it were, at the crossroads, halfway between its a priori principle which is formal and its a posteriori incentive which is material." *Critique of Practical Reason,* tr. L. W. Beck, *op. cit.*, p. 61.

the form of innocence and has become responsible through self-transcendence.[12] The will then is seen to have both an empirical and an a priori part and, as Kant says, it stands midway between the two as the ground and origin of both. The alienation here involved is prior to moral action and a necessary precondition of it. Kant was persuaded that the conflict in the will which characterizes the moral situation can be resolved within and only within the will itself. There is no possibility that the problem can be overcome through action or that action might result in a further accentuation of the split within the will.

But action poses a problem, for the will must translate itself into an act, and the action may not express the intention. Or, put in other terms, the self can achieve its freedom only through action, yet in making the self determinate the action is, in one sense, the negation of freedom. Prior to the action the self is simply a possibility. Through action it makes itself into an actuality, an objective reality. But in the process of acting it finds itself in a new mode of self-estrangement as both subject and object to itself. Kierkegaard seems quite close to Kant in insisting upon the ethico-religious nature of the problem, and the crucial fact of ultimate resolution. Like Kant he is not seriously concerned with the phenomenal, save in so far as it

[12] "Innocence is indeed a glorious thing, but, on the other hand, it is very sad that it cannot well maintain itself, being easily led astray." *Ibid.*, p. 65. But why *sad,* one may ask. If it were possible for "innocence to maintain itself," morality and duty, with its sublimity, would be impossible. In this observation, Kant seems to recognize that morality may involve a loss as well as a gain for mankind.

may be the expression of a will which either does not will itself or wills itself inadequately. At the same time he finds the possibility of authentic self-affirmation revealed even in the inauthentic manifestation of the self and treats the relation between the authentic and the inauthentic dialectically. The dialectic of absolute spirit of the Hegelian philosophy is transferred by Kierkegaard to finite spirit.[13] But unlike Hegel, the dialectic transpires within the ethico-religious will. Kierkegaard has made use of the subtleties of the Hegelian dialectical method and has enlarged the problem to include the religious, but in the final analysis he stands with Kant in holding that the dialectic can be overcome ethically only by the resolute choice of the individual will.

Almost in spite of himself Kierkegaard disclosed the importance of the dialectical relation between the authentic and inauthentic modes of subjective existence. He interiorized the Hegelian dialectic, turned the macrocosm into the microcosm, but like Kant he left us with the problem of relating the external to the internal, the phenomenal to the noumenal. It is significant that when Heidegger turned to the problem of the self and the world, operating un-

13 "The self is a relation which relates itself to its own self, or it is that in the relation [which accounts for it] that the relation relates itself to its own self; the self is not the relation but [consists in the fact] that the relation relates itself to its own self." Kierkegaard, *Sickness unto Death,* tr. A. B. Lowrie (1900), p. 146. Let those who consider Kierkegaard to be the complete and perfect antithesis of Hegel ponder this statement! It is not irony, but a concise though awkward formulation of Kierkegaard's own view of the self.

der the strong influence both of Kant and of Kierkegaard, he concluded that both self and world are necessary modes of existence and that no moral choice can be made between them. On Heidegger's analysis, the self can be brought to the authentic affirmation of itself only through the mode of unauthenticity. Being in the world, phenomenal existence, is a structural characteristic of human existence.[14] The self is related to its own fundamental being only through the mediation of its existence in the world.[15] To exist at all is to stand off from oneself, to project oneself into the world. Heidegger acknowledges the dialectical relation between the subjective and objective modes of human existence, but sees no possibility of resolution. Man's existence tends to become an inescapable oscillation between the two poles. Without God or absolute spirit, no possibility of a metaphysical resolution is available, and man is revealed as standing in a tragic situation.

Thus far we have laid great stress upon the element of subjectivity in Kant for the sake of making clear to what extent he provided one of the fundamental themes for existential philosophy. But our emphasis has been one-sided and we have left out altogether a factor which is equally important for his influence upon the existentialist thinkers. In the course of formulating his metaphysics Kant persisted in talking in a way that has bothered almost all phi-

[14] "Weil zu Dasein wesenhaft das In-der-Welt-Sein gehört, ist sein Sein zur Welt wesenhaft Besorgen." Heidegger, *Sein und Zeit* (1949), p. 57.

[15] *Ibid.*, pp. 57 ff.

losophers who have studied him or been influenced by him. He insisted on referring in many different contexts to what he called a thing-in-itself. It is a troublesome referent, for the thing-in-itself is really not a thing; in fact, it is nothing at all. Why Kant should have been so obsessed with it has remained a complete mystery to many of his most ardent disciples, and even the most charitable of them have sometimes been inclined to regard it as a perversity. It is safe to say, I think, that the doctrine of the thing-in-itself presents the single greatest stumbling block in the Kantian philosophy.

I have said that it is really *nothing,* but one might just as well say that it is *being.* And to claim respectability for this statement one might appeal to no less a philosopher than Hegel.[16] The concept of the thing-in-itself expresses in Kantian terms reality in its mode of radical transcendence. There would be no need to talk of phenomenalism or even of subjectivity in Kant's philosophy were it not for the radical transcendence of being. Although Kant was a transcendental philosopher, seeking to determine the a priori structure of our mode of cognition and action, it was always toward the transcendent that he was oriented. The "Copernican revolution," after all, does not really make man the center of the cosmos. He is thrown back upon himself, indeed, but not in such a way that the whole universe rotates around him as its pivotal center. We would misunderstand Kant's phenomenalism and his subjectivism badly if we were to think of it as anthropocentric. The real center for

[16] Cf. *Wissenschaft der Logik,* Vol. I, Einleitung.

Kant's philosophy is being-in-itself, which presents itself to us negatively in all phases of our experience. It is the absolute limit which reveals to us our finiteness and our subjectivity. It is the measure in terms of which all human standards are only relative.

Those who are at all familiar with Kant's *Critique of Pure Reason* and his *Critique of Judgment* will have little difficulty in recognizing this factor of transcendence. But it is somewhat different in the case of the *Critique of Practical Reason,* for this work is really not a "critique" and the title is a misnomer. Kant came closest to a critical analysis of practical reason in his treatment of "radical evil" in the *Religion*[17] but never carried it through to deal extensively or systematically with the ultimate limits of man's autonomy. It was Hegel rather than Kant who wrote the necessary "critique" of practical reason by establishing the limits of moral autonomy. Nor was Kant altogether unaware of at least some of these difficulties. Kant characterized his metaphysics of morals as subjective, but only for the reason that it issues in faith—and not because it is based on faith.[18] There is nothing subjective whatever about the moral law. It is binding on God and man alike.[19] One finds no genuine dialectic of the practical reason, no proper antinomies. And this is due to the fact, perhaps, that Kant failed to emphasize adequately the factor of

[17] Cassirer, VI, 201 ff.

[18] *Kritik der praktischen Vernunft,* Cassirer, V, 136 ff., 150.

[19] Though not as an imperative for God, since there is no opposition between inclination and reason in God's will. Nonetheless God's will is perfectly lawful and in its holiness embodies the "supreme principle of morality." *Ibid.,* p. 136.

transcendence as it pertains to moral experience. With characteristic judiciousness Kant often remarked that the categorical imperative must be considered *as if* it were the command of God. But it is *not* the *voice of God* and nothing could be more subjective than to regard it as such. In his treatment of religion Kant was altogether too much inclined to regard it as the voice of God, or at least the form in which God must speak to man. This much of Kant's philosophy does not seem to be in keeping with his own best insights, and Kant has provided us with the necessary instruction for correcting it.

These may seem to be harsh words and to give expression to a harsh judgment. But they are, I think, to the point, and we would do less than credit to a philosopher of Kant's stature if we were to hesitate in passing our own judgment on the adequacy of his formulations. I have called attention to this shortcoming only because of its importance for Kant's relation to the existentialist philosophers.

In a book which is sharply critical of existentialism, Helmut Kuhn has written of what he calls *The Encounter with Nothingness*.[20] In selecting this title Kuhn intended to point to the nihilistic tendencies in existential philosophy. Unfortunately he did not take adequately into account the fact that the concept of nothingness is one of the most respectable notions in Western philosophy.[21] I shall not attempt to

[20] 1951.

[21] Cf. Hegel, *Logik*, Lasson ed., p. 58. "Der Anfang enthält also beides, Sein und Nichts; ist die Einheit von Sein und Nichts;–oder ist Nichtsein, das zugleich Sein, und Sein, das zugleich Nichtsein ist."

delineate its legitimate line of descent, but content myself with what has already been said about its centrality for Kant. The correlate of subjectivity in Kant's thought is transcendence, and the subjectivity is radical in direct ratio to the radicalism of transcendence. Among the philosophers of existence one finds the same basic consciousness of ultimate reality as transcendent that one finds in Kant.

As has been suggested earlier, Kierkegaard tended to let the phenomenal world slip away altogether. He stressed the terrible isolation of the individual who is confronted with the task of deciding what to do about his own existence. But correlative with Kierkegaard's stress on the subjectivity of existence is his emphasis upon the unqualified transcendence of God. Kierkegaard's treatment of faith resulted in the negative theology of Karl Barth in which God is characterized as "wholly other." There is a double transcendence in Kierkegaard, the transcendence of the self to itself as possibility, and secondly, the transcendence of the self by God. Thus self-transcendence is itself transcended in Kierkegaard, and human autonomy qualified by the unconditioned reality of God. Kierkegaard took the self as a thing-in-itself, and in grappling with it in his own person sought to bring its depths to light. The result is a powerfully subtle analysis of self-existence which makes the work of many previous philosophers look elementary by comparison. Kierkegaard went beyond the moral to the religious, a point which Kant had barely touched. He revealed moral existence itself as but a phenomenal expression of the noumenal depths of the self. In his passionate struggle with the transcendent reality of the self and God, Kierkegaard provided a new vitality for philosophical inquiry and proved to be as revolutionary in his own way as Kant.

In spite of his own realistic and metaphysical orientation, Kant's philosophy provided a great stimulus for phenomenalism. The Hegelians, the neo-Kantians, the pragmatists, and the positivists all were phenomenalists of a sort. The positivists have retained the factor of transcendence in spite of themselves by continuing to call attention to the meaningless. This was a great mistake on their part, for the surest way to set philosophically minded individuals at work on a problem is to call it meaningless. The meaningless is also the mysterious, and philosophy flourishes on mystery. Kant's philosophy gave rise to a predominantly un-Kantian movement which was destined to develop in two opposed directions, the absolutistic and the positivistic, before reversing itself. The return to the thing-in-itself which takes the form of an encounter with nothingness is a return to the standpoint of Kant. It is nihilistic only in its repudiation of phenomenalism, and must inevitably give rise to positive and constructive developments.

That this is the case we can see most clearly in the writings of Heidegger, who is far and away the most original and important of the philosophers of existence. So far is he from being nihilistic that in his earliest work he employed a method which is scholastic in its rigor and architectonic in its structure. Heidegger was brought to the realization of the transcendence of being through Kant and Kierkegaard.

He restates Kant's question: Why is there something rather than nothing at all? and makes it the focus for his explorations. Death as the possibility of nonexistence serves to throw man back upon his own inner being. But death, for Heidegger, is symbolic of nothingness in general and serves to open the way to a new understanding of being.[22] If we are to understand being, whether it be our own or that of a thing, we must grasp it in terms of the possibility of its own nonbeing. Starting with death and its significance for human existence, Heidegger is driven back to the original problem of being and nonbeing as formulated by Parmenides and Plato.[23] By taking the Kantian doctrine of the thing-in-itself seriously, Heidegger finds himself asking once more the most fundamental questions. Initially it was through human existence alone that Heidegger hoped to gain access to being. But he came to recognize more and more that the ontological difference between being and existence is pervasive, and that one may consider a thing as well as a man for the purposes of ontological analysis.[24]

One of Heidegger's more recent essays is entitled "Das Ding." In this essay Heidegger does not approach the meaning of a thing in terms of its relation to human existence, but takes it as it is in itself. This approach appears to represent a direct reversal of his procedure in *Sein und Zeit,* for in the earlier treatment he had analyzed objects simply as tools of one

[22] *Sein und Zeit,* p. 252.

[23] *Was ist Metaphysik?* (1900), p. 25.

[24] Cf. *Einführung in die Metaphysik* (1953), pp. 60 ff.; see also F. J. von Rintelen, *Philosophie der Endlichkeit* (1951), pp. 275 ff.

sort or another and showed no interest in their intrinsic being. The shift in Heidegger's approach is significant, for it indicates the impossibility of limiting the question of being to man. Man is anxious and concerned about his own being, as both Kierkegaard and Heidegger have brought out. But it is nothing short of ridiculous to regard the world as reflecting in its structure nothing more than the characteristics of human existence. In his first book Heidegger had interpreted the world so subjectively that it failed to accord with some of our more fundamental observations about it, particularly such stubborn physical characteristics as spatial distance.[25] It is very well to say that distance is relative and a function of our concern, but it is also true that we cannot change the mileage to Boston. Heidegger came to see, I think, that his initial phenomenalistic account of the world had not taken into consideration an important facet of being—namely, that which is not our own. If taken phenomenally, the world stands between man and ultimate reality and mediates between the two. It presents man with a mirror in which to discern himself, but also in which he can find traces of transcendent reality. Kant had insisted quite rightly that the appearance is the appearance *of* a thing in itself. In calling it an *appearance* he meant to call attention both to the fact that it *appears to us* and, secondly, that it is the *appearance of something*.[26] To leave out one side of the relation is, as Heidegger discovered, a serious error. In spite of Heidegger's protestations to

[25] Cf. *Sein und Zeit,* pp. 108 ff.
[26] *Critique of Pure Reason,* Bxxvii.

the contrary, his analysis of human existence in *Sein und Zeit* must be taken as an exercise in philosophical anthropology.

In so far as the existentialist thinkers follow Kant's distinction between appearance and reality, they are committed to maintain the fact of transcendence in all elements of human experience. As has been indicated, Kant held that reason must function symbolically in attempting to represent ultimate reality. Jaspers has made much of this point with his concept of the cipher, which, in its incapacity for literal translation, serves to point beyond itself to the transcendent.[27] He develops systematically some of the ideas which Kant treated rather sketchily in the *Critique of Judgment* in discussing aesthetic ideas. Kant never attempted to develop a theory of symbols but he committed himself to the thesis that metaphysical ideas perform a symbolic function and are thus closely related to works of art.[28] We cannot move beyond experience either by the literal use of concepts or by a strict doctrine of analogy, but we can employ what Kant termed a kind of "symbolical anthropomorphism." This side of Kant's thought is little noted, and prior to Jaspers had not been developed, save in the work of Ernst Cassirer.[29] But in rejecting the thing-in-itself Cassirer lost the transcendent reference which is essential to the Kantian conception of symbolism.

[27] Karl Jaspers, *Philosophie* (1948), pp. 875 ff.

[28] *Kritik der Urteilskraft,* § 59, Cassirer, V, 428 ff.

[29] Cf. Ernst Cassirer, *The Philosophy of Symbolic Form* (1953), I, 76 ff.

One can see the way in which symbolic expression is made necessary by the stress on radical transcendence if one considers the writings of the negative theologians. They have insisted that theological truths can only be expressed in symbolical and even mythological form, for only in this way can one preserve the transcendent reference. One sees this, too, in Heidegger, who has turned increasingly to the poets for inspiration and who himself seems often to speak in poetic and symbolic language. To the degree that Heidegger holds to the *ontological difference* on which he initially insisted, this is precisely the way in which one would expect him to speak. The positivists have indicted metaphysics as a kind of poetry, but they did not mean thereby to assign to it any truth status. If Kant and the existentialist philosophers are correct, metaphysics has something in common with poetry to the extent that they both employ a symbolic mode of representation. In this same connection it may not be unimportant that Sartre combines in himself the artistic and the philosophical. His plays may express the inevitability of presenting philosophical ideas in symbolic form.

I must hasten to add that Kant is not the only major philosopher who pointed to the necessity of expressing metaphysical truths in symbolic form. Plato had, of course, made extensive use of the myth as a form for presenting some of his most important ideas. There are those who would argue that he used the mythological form only when he had not worked out his ideas in an adequate conceptual fashion, and that the myths were a convenient avenue of escape from the demands of precise thought. But there is good reason to believe that Plato's use of myths was deliberate and intended to be instructive. The similarity between Plato and Kant on this point is interestingly reflected in the writings of Jaspers, for Jaspers acknowledges that these two philosophers have been the most important for his own philosophical development. In spite of their differences Plato and Kant are in agreement on this point. The existentialists stand more in the Platonic-Kantian than in the Aristotelian-Hegelian tradition in this respect.

It should be evident from what has been said already that it is somewhat paradoxical to speak of *existential philosophy*. Kierkegaard, who is the fountainhead of the movement, was not a philosopher in the strict sense of the term, and Heidegger, the most able philosophical exponent of the movement, refuses now to be classed as an existentialist. Jaspers, too, is somewhat unhappy of late with this designation and prefers to think of himself as a "philosopher of reason." [30] He sounds more and more like Kant in his more rationalistic moments, and in his attempt to write a comprehensive logic of existence gives evidence of a certain affinity for Hegel. Marcel, too, has moved away from his earlier views and is uncomfortable at being classed as an existentialist. This would seem to leave Sartre in the position of having to defend the existentialist fort. But when Sartre finally gives us the positive side of his philosophy and his ethics, which have long been promised, he, too, will

[30] Cf. Karl Jaspers, *Vernunft und Widervernunft* (1900), Part III.

doubtless be seen to emerge from the existentialist cocoon. Where are we, then? Has our specimen vanished during the course of our dissection? Is existentialism really a position or only a moving point which refuses to be fixed?

The tendency to move from what may be called an existentialist starting point is, I think, instructive. It indicates that the *existential* is not really a philosophical system or even a firm position, but a moment, a necessary moment, in philosophical inquiry. Now that the more extreme statements of the existentialist point of view are before us, it is easy for us to see the existentialist commitment in Socrates and Plato, in Kant and Nietzsche, and even in Hegel. Soon enough we will recognize that every genuine philosopher has exhibited some grasp of existentialist principles, though some far more than others. Through magnification and exaggeration the existentialist thinkers have brought this principle to the level of full self-consciousness.

None of the major existentialist writers is actually nihilistic, with the possible exception of Sartre. And for reasons which I have just mentioned, it is not at all clear that his philosophy is fundamentally negative in its impact. In a time when men have had enough of phenomenalism and positivism, and when human reason has lost contact with its transcendent ground, the philosophy of existence offers an exciting alternative. It frankly recognizes human despair in a world which is dominated by technology and by the technical exercise of reason, and calls upon man passionately and courageously to wrestle with the problem of his own meaninglessness. There is the danger, of course, that it should serve as a surrogate for religion, a sore temptation in an age of despair. But existentialism is not on the whole a popular movement, certainly not outside France. Aside from the plays of Sartre, the writings of the existentialists are hard going indeed, as those can testify who have struggled with any one of Kierkegaard's discourses or with one of Heidegger's essays. In the long run it will be the individual philosophers rather than the movement as a whole which will be philosophically important. Schools of philosophy have a way of drying up and withering without leaving any lasting imprint upon human thought, and there is no reason to think that it will be otherwise in the case of the existentialists.

I have not attempted to make out that Kant was the *first* existentialist or even the father of existentialism. He is, however, the most important philosophical influence upon the existentialist philosophers, certainly upon Jaspers and Heidegger, and indirectly upon Kierkegaard. Two of the major themes in existentialist thought, subjectivity and transcendence, stem directly from Kant and are handled in a Kantian spirit. The stress on freedom, the primacy of the moral, and the formalism in existential philosophy are also derivative from Kant. But we must hasten to add that Kant was even more directly the progenitor of Hegelian idealism, which is taken by many to be the direct antithesis of existentialism. Kierkegaard derived his dialectical method from Hegel, and existentialism in general is deeply indebted to the

Hegelian philosophy. Sartre borrows some of his basic categories directly from Hegel, and Heidegger has relied heavily upon Plato, Aristotle, and the pre-Socratics. Only fifty years ago the idealists could claim Kant for their philosopher, even as some of the existentialists claim him today. But, like Plato, Kant is a philosopher of such magnitude that no school can claim to have developed the full substance of his thought. Finally, we must remember that Kant was fundamentally a philosopher of revolution, and only those philosophers can rightly claim to follow him who think for themselves. Philosophical orientation is not a natural endowment but, like moral character, can only be achieved by the free and resolute exercise of the human mind.

AESTHETICS AND CRITICISM

René Wellek

AESTHETICS AND CRITICISM

By René Wellek

THOMAS DE QUINCEY, the author of *Confessions of an English Opium Eater,* wrote in one of his essays that Kant was "something of a brute." "It is very evident," he says, "that Kant's original determination was a coarse, masculine pursuit of science and that literature in its finer departments . . . was to him, at all parts of his life, an object of secret contempt." Kant, he tells us, "in all probability never read a book in his life," no book of poetry or fiction, only voyages and travels and scientific treatises.[1] This image of Kant as the uncouth German pedant still lingers on and has not been completely eradicated, though a mass of evidence has been accumulated to show that it is very far from the truth. Kant's writings, lecture notes, conversations, and letters show that he had a considerable knowledge of imaginative literature, especially poetry; that he composed some occasional verses himself as a young man; and that, in his social life, he was a man of exquisite courtesy and fine manners who had great interest in the pleasures of the table and in good conversation. His taste in literature was, no doubt, old-fashioned in the Germany of the last decades of the eighteenth century when his fame and influence were at their height. We must remember that Kant was born in

[1] *Collected Writings,* ed. David Masson (1896), VIII, 90, 91, 93.

1724 and thus formed his taste in the 1740s before the great age of German literature, before the rise of Lessing, Goethe, and Schiller. Kant knew his Latin poets: even when old and feeble, he could recite long passages from Virgil and his favorite Persius.[2] He had a definite taste especially for two kinds of literature: satire and didactic, philosophical poetry. He quoted Horace and Lucretius, admired Erasmus of Rotterdam, Samuel Butler's *Hudibras,* Swift, and especially Pope's *Essay on Man.* He knew Cervantes, Montaigne, and Milton, and was swept off his feet, temporarily at least, by Rousseau. But as he grew older, he became hostile to the new literature springing up around him; he disapproved of the extravagant cult of genius in the German *Sturm und Drang* and disliked all sentimentalism; he thought the man unhappy who had a novel-reading wife. "In her imagination she was married to Sir Charles Grandison and she is now his widow. She won't have much inclination to look after things in the kitchen." [3] Kant, we must conclude, was a cultivated gentleman, well-read in the literature of the Romans and of his youth, with a taste for poetry which we should call neoclassical. He could not change or enlarge his taste, as time went on, just as most of us cling to the artistic experiences of our youth. His knowledge of the other

[2] Reported by two of Kant's earliest biographers, L. E. Borowski and E. A. C. Wasianski, in *Immanuel Kant: Sein Leben in Darstellungen von Zeitgenossen,* ed. Felix Gross (1912), pp. 78, 232 f.

[3] Quoted from lecture note by Erich Adickes in "Kant als Aesthetiker," *Jahrbuch des Freien Deutschen Hochstifts* (1904), p. 322.

arts was more limited; he had never traveled beyond the confines of East Prussia and thus had no firsthand view of great architecture or painting; it seems not surprising to hear that he liked the engravings of Hogarth best. But one can have real access to the experience of art even if only in a narrow range, and surely the fact of that experience is the only thing that mattered to Kant, or should matter to any philosopher thinking about the nature of art.

Kant was not a practical critic of the arts. In the *Critique of Judgment* he mentions only two poets, Homer and Wieland, in the same sentence, and only once does he appeal to specific poetic texts to illustrate a point: to lines from a French poem by Frederick the Great and to a metaphor in an obscure contemporary, Withof.[4] Kant was not even a philosopher of art. He says very little about the individual arts as such, and nothing about their historical development or forms. Rather he was preoccupied with two problems: aesthetics, in the narrow sense of the word as it was understood in his time to mean our response to the beautiful, and the theory of criticism—or rather with one central question: whether the judgment of taste is subjective or objective, relative or absolute. On both these problems, aesthetics and theory of criticism, Kant has things to say which seem relevant and substantially true even today.

Kant must be considered the first philosopher who clearly and definitely established the peculiarity and autonomy of the aesthetic realm. Croce claimed that Vico was the founder of aesthetics, but Vico was un-

[4] *Kritik der Urteilskraft,* Cassirer, V, 384, 391.

able to distinguish between poetry and myth and assigned poetry to the early stages of mankind, as a sort of prelogical thinking. Baumgarten, who invented the term aesthetics and wrote the first book called *Aesthetica,* published in 1750, conceived his science rather as a kind of inductive logic, a science of perception, in which, for instance, telescopes, thermometers, and barometers are treated as important instruments. Only in Kant do we find an elaborate argument that the aesthetic realm differs from the realm of morality, utility, and science because the aesthetic state of mind differs profoundly from our perception of the pleasurable, the moving, the useful, the true, and the good. Kant invented the famous thesis that the aesthetic response consists in "disinterested satisfaction." "Disinterested" in this formula refers to a lack of interference from desire, a directness in our access to the work of art. Our access is undisturbed, uninterfered with by immediate utilitarian ends.

The idea of the autonomy of art was not, of course, totally new with Kant: it was being prepared throughout the century, and anticipations can be found in thinkers such as the Scotsman Francis Hutcheson and the German-Jewish philosopher Moses Mendelssohn. But in Kant the argument was stated for the first time systematically in a defense of the aesthetic realm against all sides: against sensualism and its reduction of art to pleasure, against emotionalism and its view of art as stimulus or emotion, against the age-old moralism, which reduces art to a form of the useful, and against intellectualism, which sees in art only an inferior, more popular way of knowing, a kind of second-rate (because less systematic) philosophy. Many attempts have been made to refute Kant's conclusions. Whatever the difficulties of Kant's solution, he has put his finger on the central issue of aesthetics. No science is possible which does not have its distinct object. If art is simply pleasure, or communication of emotion, or experience, or inferior reasoning, it ceases to be art and becomes a substitute for something else.

Art or the beautiful is not pleasure because pleasure is something purely subjective, not referable to an object: pleasure can never err or be false. Pleasure is momentary, it is consumed, it ceases after being satisfied. But aesthetic contemplation is, as if arrested in time, repeatable, though free from desire. Pleasure or pain accompanies all our actions, but pleasure does not set off the realm of the aesthetic. The tragic or the grotesque or the ugly depicted in art may even be painful in the ordinary sense of the word.

Art is not good or useful either. It does not serve an immediate purpose, it does not arouse a desire to consume or use it. Kant's view does not, as we shall see, preclude the moral significance of art. What mattered to him was the special nature of art, the way we would say aesthetic experience is "framed," is distanced, is set off from the feelings of desire and willing. He wanted to distinguish the whole world of illusion which is created by art and demands another attitude than that of immediate use or consumption.

Nor is the aesthetic state of mind an inferior way to abstract knowledge. Kant does not always carefully enough guard against an intellectualistic misinterpretation. On the whole he understands the danger clearly, but one of the key terms which he introduces, his "aesthetic Idea," raises many difficulties. This "Idea," he knows, is not identical with general idea or concept. An aesthetic Idea is a representation of the imagination which has the semblance of reality. The term "Idea" is near to the term "symbol," which was introduced in its modern meaning to aesthetics by Goethe and Schiller. "Idea" points to a pervasive problem of Kant's *Critique,* the union of the general and the particular, the abstract and the sensuous, achieved by art.

The aesthetic realm is thus that of imagination, not of thought, or goodness, or utility, but of imagination represented, objectified, symbolized, distanced, contemplated. However we rephrase it, it seems to me that Kant has clearly grasped the nature of the aesthetic and the realm of art.

He has stated with equal clarity and has answered the central question concerning a theory of criticism. Kant speaks of the judgment of "taste." The term "taste" was first applied to things of the mind in the seventeenth century, but elicited a considerable debate only in the eighteenth century, when Montesquieu, Voltaire, Hume, and Burke took a prominent part. There were two conceptions of "taste" with which Kant was confronted and which, in different forms, are still debated today. One group of thinkers answered that taste is simply another sense, a sixth sense, completely irrational, something, as we should say, purely subjective. As the old saying runs, *de gustibus non est disputandum.*

But another group argued that taste is the discovery of objective principles, or rules, or laws, and that it differs from the process of reasoning only by being quicker and surer, a kind of short cut possible because of training and exercise. We recognize things better if we have seen them before and know what others found in them: taste is merely a knowledge of principles and rules, an acceptance of the wisdom and verdict of the ages.

Kant begins with this dilemma; he is quite familiar with this dispute. He holds firm to the subjective side of the argument, recognizing that judgments of taste, our pleasure or boredom, can neither be refuted nor enforced. He rejects any view of criticism by a priori principles, by laws or rules. Kant argues elaborately that it is quite true that taste is subjective; yet aesthetic judgments differ from a taste, say, in olives or oysters, by claiming universality. If it were like a taste in olives nobody could or would argue about works of art. On the other hand, if aesthetic judgment were an appeal to laws or eternal principles all argument would stop, too. It would be merely a question of application. We should not need to collect examples, any more than we need to collect examples of the law of gravity; *all* things fall. The aesthetic judgment is rather something in between. It is subjective, but there is an objectivity in the subjective: in the aesthetic judgment egoism is overcome: we appeal to a general judgment, to a common sense of mankind, but this is achieved by inner experience, not by accepting the opinions of others or consulting them or counting their opinions.

It is not an appeal to men, but an appeal to humanity, to an ideal totality of judges. I cannot know whether I have actually, in my judgment, hit on the sentiment of this hidden ideal totality, yet my aesthetic judgment is a pointing to this higher unity, a call to myself and others to discover it. It is thus hypothetical, problematical. To rephrase this in modern terms, aesthetic judgment is neither relative nor absolute: it is neither completely individual, as this would mean an anarchy and a complete frustration of criticism, nor is it absolute in the sense that we can apply established, eternal norms. Criticism is personal but it aims to discover a structure of determination in the object itself: it assumes some standard of correctness in the judgment even though we may not be able to draw the exact line between the subjective and the objective in each given instance. Kant, it seems to me, succeeds in avoiding both of two extremes which have at different times paralyzed criticism: anarchic subjectivity and frozen absolutism. While Kant recognizes the role of personal feeling in art, he sees that there is paradoxically something like an aesthetic duty. Nobody ought to like olives but all of us *should* respond to great art and distinguish between the good and the bad if we are to be fully human. Still the aesthetic "ought" is by no means the same as the ethical "ought," Kant's categorical imperative, which demands action from every man without distinction, at any time and in any place. The aesthetic duty, paradoxically, is only subjective and contemplative.

In Kant there cannot be any rules or laws of art

which are given a priori. Thus Kant quite logically (though one may be surprised at this) makes much of original genius. We must not, of course, think that Kant's genius is the egotistical superman he became in the hands of certain Romantics, or the savage, inspired creature he had become during Kant's own lifetime among the geniuses of *Sturm und Drang*. Kant's concept of genius is exactly parallel to his concept of judgment. He recognizes in genius a basic irrationality; the source of genius is in the unconscious. Genius is innate, a gift of nature. It cannot invent general prescriptions for works of art, as this would make art the application of precepts and concepts; it is always original genius. But there can be, of course, original nonsense (just as there can be nonsensical, false judgments of taste). Hence the products of genius must be "exemplary," normative, prescriptive, as true taste is prescriptive. Genius is the "talent by which nature prescribes rules to art." [5] Works of art claim recognition, and the critic has the duty to give it to them.

But how precisely can criticism proceed? For Kant there cannot be anything like a doctrine or principles which can be taught. Criticism is always judging by examples, from the concrete. Criticism thus is historical, in the sense of being individual, while science (and Kant thinks of physical science) is general, abstract, aiming at a systematic doctrine. The method of criticism is thus the comparative method. The capacity to choose with universal validity, another definition of taste, is nothing but the capacity of comparing

[5] *Ibid.*, p. 382.

oneself with others; and that process is, of course, not just a juxtaposition with others, but a self-criticism, an introspection, an examination of one's feelings.

I personally think that Kant leaves us too much in the realm of the subjective: I recognize, of course, that this agrees with his general position on the theory of knowledge. Kant rarely comes to grips with the concrete realm of art. Poetry as such is hardly treated in the *Critique* except in the classification of the arts, where it is listed as an "art of speech" with rhetoric and put first among the arts, because it liberates the imagination and rises to "ideas."[6] But Kant did suggest or rather revive a very important criterion for the judgment of art: the analogy of the organism. The similarity of a work of art to an organism was, I believe, first suggested in a famous passage of Aristotle's *Poetics,* but there it is simply a principle of wholeness, a recognition of the implication of the parts in a whole, a totality or unity: the organistic analogy had been only a variety of the old insight that a work of art is a unity in diversity. But in Kant we are confronted with a different idea: art and nature are conceived as much stricter analogies. The work of art is parallel to a living organism because art and organic nature must both be conceived under the head of what Kant calls paradoxically "purposeless purposiveness." The *Critique of Judgment* has two parts: the "Critique of Aesthetic Judgment" and the "Critique of Teleological Judgment"; one is concerned with what we call aesthetics and art, the other with what we should call biology, or rather

[6] *Ibid.,* p. 402.

the theory of biology. This is not, as some people have thought, an odd scholastic scheme which brings incompatibles under one artificial heading: it is a central insight of Kant's philosophy. Art and organic nature point to an ultimate overcoming of the deep dualism which is basic to Kant's system of thought. The world, according to Kant, is divided into two realms; that of appearance (hence of necessity, of physical causality), accessible to our senses and the categories of our understanding, and that of moral freedom, accessible only in action. Kant glimpses in art a possibility of bridging the gulf between necessity and freedom, between the world of deterministic nature and the world of moral action. Art accomplishes a union of the general and the particular, of intuition and thought, of imagination and reason. Organic nature, life, does exactly the same. They together guarantee the existence of what Kant calls the "supersensuous," for only in art and life, through "intellectual intuition," do we have access to what Kant calls the "intellectual archetype." [7] To put this in more modern terms: art and life point to some realm of values, or ends, or purposes, discernible in the activity of genius, in our response to beauty, and in the purposeful structures of living beings. But Kant hesitates to come to this conclusion: the "supersensuous substratum of nature," the union of the realm of necessity and freedom, escapes, he would insist, any *theoretical* knowledge. Hegel, who boldly proclaimed the reality of the spirit, was to complain about Kant: "It is the character of Kant's philosophy

[7] *Ibid.*, p. 487.

to have a consciousness of the highest idea, but always to eradicate it again." [8] But while Kant hesitates to assign to art the role of mediatress between man and nature, he discovers and correctly emphasizes a most important criterion of aesthetic judgment: the analogy between art and organism. The term "purposeless purposiveness" as applied to organism becomes clear if we understand that by "purpose" Kant does not mean conscious intention and aim, but harmony of parts, unity, totality, with every member having its own proper function in the system. This purposiveness, this unity, is at the same time purposeless in Kant's sense, as it is disinterested, not directed to any immediate outside aim. Such coherence in itself, such beautiful unity, is also a standard of aesthetic judgment: the more complex the work of art, the more composed, the greater the totality, the greater the beauty. Thus Kant, while envisaging the analogy between nature and art as of great philosophical importance, does not go all the way in identifying art with organism. He knew the difference and always insisted that creatures are subject to the laws of causality and physics; while works of art are not, because they are illusion, semblance, make-believe.

One other motif of Kant's aesthetics proved of great historical importance. Kant inherited from the eighteenth century the division of the aesthetic realm into the beautiful and the sublime. The distinction seems to me untenable in its rigidity, but Kant's theory of the sublime, though applied by him exclusively to nature, could easily be and soon was trans-

[8] *Sämtliche Werke* (1832-44), XVI, 127.

ferred to tragedy. The sublime is frightening, upsetting, even horrifying, but at the same time attractive. Man in the experience of the sublime in nature confronts either magnitude or power, both of which transcend the capabilities of his imagination. While beauty induces sensibility and understanding to collaborate harmoniously, sublimity causes a conflict between imagination and reason. Our imagination fails to grasp the infinity of the universe or the omnipotence of nature displayed in storms, earthquakes, and other natural catastrophes. But while we experience our impotence before nature, we still assert our humanity, a sense of our freedom, of our supersensuous destiny. Thus the sublime proves to be another road to the supersensuous, not, of course, grasped by reason, but glimpsed merely by imagination. If we apply the sublime to art (as Kant did not explicitly), we have found another way to give metaphysical and moral meaning to art. Kant himself hesitates, for he sees in sublimity a hint of man's freedom from the natural order of the universe. A theory which starts with a sharp delimitation of the aesthetic, if then stretched so as to unite the aesthetic and the sublime, will end with a justification for the greatest metaphysical and moral claims for art. In Kant these claims are put forward hesitatingly, gropingly, cautiously, as suits his temperament and critical method.

One may look upon the whole history of general aesthetics after Kant as a series of discussions, repudiations, and developments of Kant's thought. I have purposely ignored or minimized the systematic exposition, the scholastic divisions and subdivisions, the whole elaborate argumentation of Kant's *Critique.* I have ignored, for instance, the awkward distinction between free and adherent beauty. Hardly anybody has preserved the exact architecture of Kant's thought. But all the main motifs and solutions propounded by Kant have proved extremely influential and fruitful.

The idea of the autonomy of art was almost immediately taken up by Kant's first distinguished pupil in aesthetics, the poet Schiller. Schiller resolutely embraces Kant's doctrine of the distinctness and apartness of the aesthetic realm. In some of his formulations he seems to come near to that idea of art for art's sake of which he has been claimed one of the main progenitors. But to see him in this way is a gross misunderstanding of Schiller's actual point of view and of the unfortunate and misleading term "play" which he borrows from Kant in describing the free aesthetic activity. Play has, for Schiller, nothing to do with the lack of consequence, the frivolity and unreality of a child's game. It is a term which designates the artist's freedom from immediate practical purposes, from utilitarian and moral considerations: his creativity, his self-activity. More resolutely than Kant, Schiller conceives the artist as a mediator between man and nature, between intellect and sense. Art, in Schiller, assumes an enormous civilizing role, described in his *Letters on the Aesthetic Education of Man* (1795). It heals the wounds of civilization, the split between man and nature, and between man's intellect and his senses. Art makes man whole again, reconciles him with the world and with himself. But the world of art is a world of illusion, of semblance, of *Schein,* a term with Neoplatonic overtones of light and luminosity as well as illusion. It was used by Kant only casually twice, I believe, in the *Critique.*[9]

While Schiller held fast to the principle of the autonomy of art, the German Romantics again blurred all distinctions. Schelling, the most important aesthetician in the succession of Kant, Fichte, Schelling, and Hegel, makes art or poetry really an all-embracing, all-conquering term in which all distinctions disappear. In the program of his philosophy which Schelling drew up in 1796, at the age of twenty-one, the philosopher is told to have as much aesthetic power as the poet. "There is no philosophy or history any more; poetry alone will outlive all other sciences and arts." [10] This claim for the pre-eminence of art must not, of course, be confused with later nineteenth-century aestheticism; it is rather an attempt to abolish all distinctions between art, religion, philosophy, and myth. While Kant was at great pains to distinguish between the good, the true, and the beautiful, Schelling exalts beauty as the highest value, and his beauty is actually truth and goodness in disguise. The same identification of art with religion and phi-

[9] *Kritik der Urteilskraft,* Cassirer, V, 402-403, 411.

[10] "Das älteste Systemprogramm des deutschen Idealismus," in Friedrich Hölderlin, *Sämtliche Werke,* ed. L. von Pigenot (3d ed., 1943), III, 623-625. I accept the view that this manuscript was composed by Schelling and not by Hölderlin. Cf. Ludwig Strauss, "Hölderlins Anteil an Schellings frühem Systemprogramm," *Deutsche Vierteljahrsschrift für Literaturwissenschaft und Geistesgeschichte,* V (1927), 679-747.

losophy is even more explicit in Novalis and in the later stages of Friedrich Schlegel's speculations. Among the German Romantics, only the sober mind of August Wilhelm Schlegel, though he criticized Kant severely for his hesitations and cautions,[11] holds fast, for the most part, to the principle of aestheic autonomy. Hegel knows the peculiar nature of art, but is unable to hold to it steadily: he often identifies it with myth or sees it as a mere steppingstone to religion and philosophy. Among the German philosophers, Schopenhauer seems to have most clearly kept to the Kantian distinction of the aesthetic realm, but with him it often becomes intellectualized. The disinterested will-less contemplation of ideas becomes only a version of the philosopher's contemplation of the universe. On the whole, the great movement of German thought after Kant's *Critiques* rather tended to weaken the distinctness of the realm of aesthetics and more and more made art a short cut to the absolute, a popular version of philosophy. Art was exalted but at the price of being lost in the Platonic triad of the beautiful, the good, and the true.

The principle of the autonomy of art was picked up by Victor Cousin and other popularizers of German philosophical thought in what is known as the "art-for-art's-sake" movement in France. This term was used, apparently for the first time, by Benjamin Constant with reference to Kant's aesthetics in his *Intimate Diary* in 1804.[12] It became a prominent slo-

[11] *Vorlesungen über schöne Literatur und Kunst,* ed. J. Minor (1884), I, 64-89.

[12] *Journaux intimes,* ed. A. Roulin and C. Roth (1952), p. 58.

gan, particularly with Gautier and Flaubert. Gautier, for instance, praised Baudelaire because he had "defended the absolute autonomy of art and would not allow poetry to have any other purpose than itself, or any task other than that of arousing in the reader's heart a sense of the beautiful in the absolute meaning of the word." [13] But in Gautier and his pupil Wilde, of course, "art for art's sake" is not so much an expression asserting the autonomy of art as a polemical weapon against the social and didactic demands of the middle-class society surrounding them: autonomy of art becomes something Kant would never have dreamed of, an assertion of the superiority of the artist to the Philistine, a proclamation of his hostility to the society in which he lives and which he has long ago given up the hope of reforming or changing in his own image. The ivory tower—a term we owe, I believe, to Vigny—or the symbolist theories about absolute or pure poetry, whether of Mallarmé or Valéry, have little to do with Kant's concept of the autonomy of art.

The Kantian point of view still is an issue in the philosophical literature of aesthetics and was restated most persuasively by Croce in his *Estetica* (1902). Croce, like Kant, sharply distinguishes art from pleasure, utility, and conceptual knowledge, but, unlike Kant, extends its realm to the whole of language and to any intuitive activity of man. Croce criticizes Kant rather severely for what he considers his intellectualism, his final surrender to the view that the aesthetic "Idea" is really only a sensuous concept, but he holds

[13] *Portraits et souvenirs littéraires* (1892), p. 182.

firm to Kant's concept of the autonomy of art. Many modern aestheticians have restated the same concept in different terms. Others, such as Santayana, Dewey, and Richards, have attacked it, and have again tried to identify art with pleasure, with emotion, or with experience in general. Kant's delimitation of the aesthetic realm has proved the leading motif of modern aesthetics, the central issue which will again and again divide and unite minds of the most different tastes and persuasions.

It is different with Kant's answer to the problem of criticism: if one looks at the history of aesthetics there can be little doubt that subjectivism and relativism have been victorious, at least since the general dissolution of German idealism after the death of Hegel. The victory of relativism has been due not only to philosophical motives but to the enormous spread of the historical point of view, and even simply to our growing knowledge of the inexhaustible variety of the world's kinds of art both in space and time. Today we seem to like and admire everything: Negro sculpture and Bach, cavemen's paintings and T. S. Eliot. On the other side of the iron curtain Marxist dialectical materialism has erected relativism and historicism into a scientific system which, by a dialectical reversal, amounts in practice to a new dogmatism. In the Western world, in recent decades, there are more and more assertions of a new faith in objective critical principles, but most of them seem to come from outside aesthetics: from T. S. Eliot's religious assumptions or from Thomism. Attempts to found a new theory of the arts based on objective universal principles are rare, or, if they are made, usually amount only to the assertion of a specific individual taste or the taste of a particular group which is defending itself and erecting its demands into laws. They have to be classified as dogmatism in Kant's sense: his peculiar in-between solution which recognizes the subjectivity of taste and still demands a world of norms which we approach from different radii—a kind of "perspectivism," as I have tried to name this view—has hardly been formulated with theoretical clarity.

Kant's analogy between art and nature was also extremely influential in his time. Goethe, Schelling, and the Schlegels threw Kant's caution to the winds and spoke boldly of a work of art as if it were a plant or an animal grown and not made—procreated, begotten, not planned and constructed. Goethe admired the *Critique of Judgment* greatly, studied it diligently and asserted that he owed to it "a most joyful epoch" in his life.[14] He was pleased to see that poetry and comparative natural science were so closely related. But Kant, of course, would not have drawn Goethe's conclusion that "a work of art must be treated as a work of nature and a work of nature as a work of art."[15] In Schelling, art also appears as an analogue of nature and of nature's creative powers. Art constitutes an active link between the soul and nature. Art does not imitate nature but has to compete with the creative power of nature, "the spirit of

[14] "Einwirkung der neueren Philosophie" (1820) in *Sämtliche Werke,* ed. E. von der Hellen (1902-7), XXXIX, 31.

[15] "Kampagne in Frankreich" (1792), *ibid.,* XXVIII, 122.

nature which speaks to us only in symbols." A work of art expresses the essence of nature and is excellent in the degree to which it shows us "this original power of nature's creation and activity." [16] The poet is, as it were, the liberator of nature and, as Novalis said of man in general, the messiah of nature.

We have, I think, ceased to understand these ideas: we do not believe in such a humanization of nature and naturalization of art. During the nineteenth and twentieth centuries the gulf between man and nature has grown in theory, and the particular use of "nature" as the ideal general state of man, which in Kant is still central, has disappeared. Kant's grouping of biology and art under one cover has long since been felt to be an artificial requirement of his systematic thought.

At the same time, the more special idea of art as organism, partly Kantian in origin, has had a great success in the modern world. The German Romantics are full of it. August Wilhelm Schlegel formulated the difference between the organic and the mechanical with special skill, and his formulas were taken over by Coleridge. Today in the English-speaking world the term "organism" as applied to art is associated with Coleridge and has been widely revived in recent decades. Not only the American "new critics" but also Croce and many Germans can be described as propounders of this parallelism which, I feel,

[16] "Über das Verhältnis der bildenden Künste zu der Natur" (1807) in *Sämtliche Werke,* ed. K. F. A. Schelling (1856-61), VII, 300 f.

should not be pressed too far and certainly leads only to misleading analogies if taken too literally.

Almost as successful was Kant's definition of the aesthetic Idea, of the peculiar union of the individual and the general, the concrete and the universal. Shortly after the *Critique* Goethe discovered the word "symbol" for this union, and after him many German aestheticians—Schelling, the Schlegels, Hegel, and others—elaborated, sometimes with a different terminology, the distinction between allegory and symbol, between aesthetic idea and concept. Art is the "sensuous shining of the Idea," according to Hegel. But in Hegelianism, Idea soon assumed merely the meaning of general concept, and much German and other nineteenth-century criticism became a hunt for central ideas, for capsule formulas, for abstract philosophical or moral messages. At the same time the concrete universal, more clearly described in Hegel than in Kant, and the concept of symbol penetrated almost everywhere: Coleridge picked it up from Goethe, the Schlegels, and Schelling; so did Carlyle, and their version of symbolism or idealism became most important for Emerson and Poe. From all kinds of sources, from the German Romantics, especially Hoffmann and Heine, from Poe and Carlyle, the concept of the artistic symbol arrived in France and led there to an aesthetic theory, that of the French symbolists, expressly centered around this concept. The French, of course, like some of their precursors, had moved far away from the Kantian source: symbol becomes with them often nothing but a mystical cipher, a dim shadow or suggestion of the supernatural world. But whatever the fortunes of the term "symbol" or "idea," the union of the particular and the general, the "concrete universal" has been recognized increasingly as the central structure of all art. After the vague mystical use of the symbolists, "symbol" has become again the object of philosophical and aesthetic speculations—in Cassirer's *Philosophy of Symbolic Forms,* for instance, or in Suzanne Langer's *Feeling and Form,* to name two authors who recognize an explicit debt to Kant and his immediate pupil, Schiller.

There is, I suppose, least to be said in favor of Kant's concept of the sublime. Most aestheticians have given up the concept and have rejected its implied division of the realm of art. Kant can rightly be criticized for defining the beautiful far too narrowly, in terms of an abstract neoclassicism. In some of his reflections Kant is surely in danger of falling into an extreme formalism. He emphasizes, for instance, design in the fine arts and would apparently dispense with color as a mere sensual stimulus. He thinks of music as only a play of sounds. In the concept of the sublime Kant found a way out of such formalism but surely found it only at the expense of consistency and coherence. Kant's view of the sublime was, however, immediately important, as it suggested the theory of tragedy formulated by Schiller and August Wilhelm Schlegel. They were paraphrasing Kant's theory of the sublime when they said that tragedy shows man's revolt against the necessity of nature, in which he perishes physically, though he triumphs spiritually. We may feel that Schiller and Schlegel have described only one kind of tragedy, but it seems an important central kind. To me this formula is more illuminating than Aristotle's obscure view of purgation and more convincing than the Hegelian concept of tragedy as that of a reconciliation of two equal moral forces. In English, A. C. Bradley's exposition of Hegel's view seems to have carried the day, but the Kantian view should appeal to those who are not content with a simple justification of the ways of God to man.

Whatever our judgment about special points of Kant's aesthetics may be, enough has been said to prove its enormous fertility and influence. Yet I should not want to stake out a claim for attention to Kant merely on historical grounds, merely in terms of his widespread influence and his role of initiator. The specific solutions given by Kant to aesthetic problems are alive and important even today. The autonomy of art is a vital issue today, and I would argue that Kant has seen it rightly: with his grasp of the distinctness of the realm of art and of the truth that it must not be confused with pleasure or utility or knowledge or even with intuition and experience in general. I am not so sure that Kant's solution of the problem of criticism does not suffer from his general emphasis on the subjective and the phenomenological. Personally, I would launch out more boldly into a realm of objective structures, into the world of existing art objects. Kant cautiously stays with the indubitable fact of the subjective judgment and only hesitatingly and provisionally appeals to some final common sense of man. Today we probably do not know what to do with the idea of the reconciliation between man and nature by art. We must put the civilizing function of art in different terms. But we must acknowledge the significance of conceiving some parallelism between a work of art and an organism. Surely one of the criteria of all art is some kind of unity in diversity, some kind of coherence, wholeness, or whatever else one may wish to call it. Kant's view of the relation between particularity and universality seems also right even today. The emphasis on the particular during the last hundred years or so has gone too far: it has cut off art from a universal meaning and driven it into the minutiae of local-color descriptions, naturalistic detail, or the private, introspective worlds of the psychological novel. We are not likely to return to the abstract neoclassicism against which the emphasis on the particular was an overviolent reaction. The recognition of both the individuality of a work of art and its universal significance, in terms such as "concrete universal" or "symbol," has become more and more prevalent.

Kant, we may conclude, is the founder of modern aesthetics. He has put clearly some of the central problems to which aesthetic thinking will have to return: the question of the autonomy of art, the problem of criticism, its subjectivity or objectivity, the relation of nature and art, the organicity of the work of art, the relation between the particular and the general in art, reconciled by Kant in what he calls "Idea" and what we would prefer to call "symbol," and finally the character of the sublime which has been applied to the theory of tragedy. In aesthetics and criticism, Kant decidedly has something to say to this age, 165 years after the publication of his *Critique of Judgment.*

FREEDOM, DEMOCRACY, AND PEACE

Charles W. Hendel

FREEDOM, DEMOCRACY, AND PEACE

By Charles W. Hendel

"No free government, or the blessings of liberty, can be preserved to any people, but by a firm adherence to justice, moderation, temperance, frugality, and virtue, and by frequent recurrence to fundamental principles."

A daily reminder of this injunction of "frequent recurrence to fundamental principles" contained in the Virginia Bill of Rights of 1776 is carried at the head of the editorial column of the *Rutland Herald*, quoting a similar statement from the Constitution of Vermont of 1777.[1] The free men of Vermont had made the previous declaration of Virginia their own resolve and incorporated it in their constitution. The Virginians, however, had not by any means been the first to declare this maxim of political wisdom. It had been stated very succinctly by the philosopher David Hume in a political work which American statesmen of that time would hardly have failed to notice, an essay entitled "The Idea of a Perfect Commonwealth," the final essay in Hume's most widely known work, the *Political Discourses* (1752). But Hume's own sentence came from a more famous, even notori-

[1] The passage in the Vermont constitution reads as follows: "Frequent recurrence to fundamental principles and a firm adherence to justice, moderation, temperance, industry and frugality are absolutely necessary to preserve the blessings of liberty and keep government free."

ous, student of politics—none other than Machiavelli: "A government," says Machiavelli, "must often be brought back to its original principles." [2] Now the "original principles" of the particular form of government which the Americans were trying to establish from 1776 onward, a "free government" and a republic, had been "frequently discussed" and indeed even fought for in a revolutionary war by the Puritans in England a century before. The men who attempted that Puritan Revolution formulated "agreements of the people" and "instruments of government" and, in effect, bills of rights defining the liberties of men in a free society. It was in part from these documents that the American statesmen drew when they drafted their declarations of rights, as in Virginia and later in the first amendments to the Constitution of the United States. They not only took over the theory of freedom but carried on the practice of free discussion which enabled them to find and devise such excellent statements of their principles of government. The values of "frequent recourse" to discussion of principles Hume had celebrated in his *History of England* and *Political Discourses,* where he only repeated and more sharply defined that tradition of English liberty, drawing a salutary lesson from "experience and history." Thus Hume was not regarded by the Americans who drew up the constitutions of their states as a mere theoretican but as a practical "politician"—a term which then had the

[2] *David Hume's Political Essays,* ed. Charles W. Hendel (New York: The Liberal Arts Press, 1953), p. 147; see also pp. i-ix, xxiv-xxvii.

honorific meaning of statesman. They in turn repeated Hume's maxim that men must frequently have recourse to the original and fundamental principles of government if they would remain free—a maxim writ large "for themselves and their posterity" in the Virginia declaration.

I have taken that historic passage from the Virginia Bill of Rights as the motto of this lecture, indicating what sort of relevance the philosophy of Kant has for us in our present world. The preamble, as it were, which I have just given, this brief sketch of the derivation and significance of the passage quoted, contains several motifs in the following "argument." But our concern will be not only with Kant's philosophical argument concerning freedom, democracy, and peace, but with his own actual example as a philosopher who would also be a citizen and who demonstrated in the circumstances of his own day how necessary and important it is at any time that men should have recourse to fundamental principles.

The most important years of Kant's long life were spent during a period marked by the two historic revolutions, the American War of Independence and the French Revolution. In the course of the years 1770 to 1781 Kant was engrossed with his epoch-making *Critique of Pure Reason.* The third of his critiques of reason, the *Critique of Judgment,* was being finished in the very year of the French Revolution.

Though he was much preoccupied with his own revolution and reconstruction in philosophy, Kant was by no means oblivious of those momentous political events. His distinguished pupil Herder, who was himself an imaginative interpreter of the meaning of history, has given detailed testimony about Kant's alertness and attention to current and world affairs. "His lecture," said Herder, "was the most entertaining conversation. With the same genius with which he criticized Leibniz and Hume, and expounded the laws of Newton and Kepler, he would also take up the writings of Rousseau or any recent discovery in nature, give his estimate of them, and come back again to the knowledge of nature and the moral worth of man. Natural history, natural philosophy, the history of nations and human nature, mathematics, and experience—these were the sources from which he enlivened his lecture. . . . Nothing worth knowing was indifferent to him." [3]

Was American news of interest to Kant, and was he in possession of any? Here is a letter of December 31, 1782, to Dr. Metzger in Königsberg. There had been some discussion in the "Göttingen Times" of an epidemic raging in Europe. As a student of physical geography, a subject on which he lectured at the university, Kant had expressed the opinion that the epidemic might have come to Europe by way of the ocean current along the west coast of North America, passing the Kurile Islands which the Russians had begun to visit. And he added as an aside on epidemics: "In the English papers several weeks ago there was a news item making much of an epidemic of influenza in September which had run through the English

[3] *Kant's Theory of Ethics,* tr. T. K. Abbott (1900), pp. xxx-xxxi.

colonies and spread to Philadelphia."[4] Five years later Philadelphia was again to be in the public eye when the great Convention met there to work out the form of federal union which should establish the still very precarious United States of America on a firm footing among the states of the world. It seems quite reasonable to infer that Kant would have paid some attention to such later news about America, in view of what we know otherwise about his lively interest in the new politics of that century.

A German scholar, Karl Vorländer, asserted in his edition of Kant's shorter writings on ethics, politics, and history: "Kant's interest in politics was stirred by the American War of Independence (1775-1783) and it was even more powerfully affected, of course, by the French Revolution."[5] From 1784 onward Kant was writing various essays on the timely problems of his contemporary world; for him philosophy was intended to be practical.

It is of this practical philosophy that I shall speak. The term "practical" means that it is philosophy dealing with man's conduct in the actual circumstance of his life, and, more particularly, with the actions wherein man's own will can have a determining role.

An example of such employment of "will" is the very pursuit of happiness itself. Here man holds to a rational course leading to some distant end; doing this requires will. Another example is conduct where

[4] Cassirer, IX, 211.
[5] Vorländer, VI, xxiv.

man acts to realize something morally imperative, as being absolutely good here and now without reference to ulterior consequences—such decision, too, is an act of will, the moral will. Then there is the broad scene of human society where the lives of people are apparently regulated by the laws of the state—yet a state can only keep order, not create it in the first place, for true order in the relationships of men comes about only when they obey the laws because the laws express their own will; it is that will of theirs, which is at once free and social, that Rousseau had called the "general will," a conception which Kant adopted as his own. Here are three examples exhibiting the important role of man's will or his "practical reason."

The character of the will in these instances cited is worth examining. The will appears to be a free agency and ruling power in man. Moreover, this will, though free, is itself governed by a rule which is not an external law but rather an inner law of the will itself. This free and self-ruling will is then not an arbitrary will but one that operates according to a law which is necessary and objective. This objectivity in turn warrants our calling the will essentially a rational will. And since this will really determines man's conduct in some degree—whether he is seeking happiness or deciding a moral act or conducting his life out of respect for the laws of his community—we here witness reason actually exerting a significant power in the direction of human behavior.

This is what Kant's practical philosophy is about—this reason that has causal efficacy, that can determine man's personal and social behavior and impart the character of objective lawfulness to it, this "practical reason."

Kant had a deep and abiding conviction about the power and authority of reason. But that practical role of reason was matched by another role, the theoretical function of reason, the power it has of determining the objective truth of phenomena. "Two things fill the mind of man with awe, the starry skies above and the moral law within." And the awed mind, responsive, both seeks to know the law of that overarching nature and to practice the moral law within.

Kant started with such convictions about reason's competence in scientific knowledge and in the moral conduct of life. There were other possible realms of achievement, too, where reason might be even more creative than in natural science and morality—as in art. There seemed indeed to be no limit to the possibilities of reason in human experience.

But Kant was a true and honest philosopher: it was his duty to question and to justify his convictions and even his very enthusiasm for reason. A letter to his friend and pupil Herz tells how critically he worked:

> One cannot force an insight into the materials one has at hand, nor hurry it by strenuous effort. Quite a long time is needed, with some intervals of respite, so as to examine one's idea in every possible aspect and in the widest context, and above all, during those quiet times when one is not actively working, he ought to let the skeptical spirit in himself come alive so that whatever he may have already thought out is then exposed to the sharpest

> probings of doubt . . . . The very recreations one takes ought to be of the kind that maintain the mind in a state of openness to suggestion and readiness to envisage the object from other sides and to extend the view from that of a microscopic examination to a broad survey and take in all conceivable points of view of the matter.[6]

And indeed the skeptical spirit in Kant was given ample scope, with the consequence that he found himself facing a crisis which had to be decided before he could retain his confidence in reason and the possibility of any future metaphysic. He then had to make a thoroughgoing critique of reason which took years longer than he had ever dreamed. Month after month and year after year he labored at his critique, for nine years. At times he wondered, as he put it, whether he could ever remove "this stone blocking my way." He yearned to be going forward with his constructive philosophy. But the skeptical questioning had first to be properly met with a "critical" solution, not with merely dogmatic affirmation of his faith.

What was that stone that blocked his way? In a letter to Garve he writes:

> I started out in my work on the *Critique* from the antinomy of pure reason. For example, the world has a beginning; it has no beginning; and so forth through the fourth antinomy. There is freedom in man, and contrariwise there is no freedom but everything takes place by natural necessity—these were the things that first awakened me from my dogmatic slumber and drove me to the critique of

[6] Cassirer, IX, 97, 105-6.

reason in order to remove the scandal of reason because it seemed to be in contradiction with itself.[7]

When reason simply follows its own inner law of thought, it appears to reach two opposite and contradictory determinations of truth. This fact of antinomy had raised the radical doubt about the integrity of pure reason. If reason can pronounce one thing to be a necessary law and then another to be equally necessary which is in absolute opposition to the first, what sort of reason is this that legislates such contradiction? And can reason thus compromised ever pretend to give any rational decision between its own equal but opposite laws? Is not reason plainly doomed to an endless tossing back and forth in dialectic as metaphysics has often shown us? What faith can there be in pure reason, unless it can be exonerated from this inner scandal?

Another matter of deep concern to Kant was equally involved, his belief in the freedom of man. There are the discoverable laws of nature, laws universal and necessary; but man is a part of nature, and consequently all his actions, including his acts of will, come under natural laws and appear necessitated. Yet man as a moral being acts as if he were free, as if his own will expressed a genuine spontaneity in himself. How could this conviction of the freedom of man be reconciled with the causal necessity of nature? The antinomy of pure reason exhibited a clear contradiction here—as well as reason's own helplessness in the face of it. So the faith in man's freedom

[7] Cassirer, X, 352.

was at stake as well as that in reason. This double concern sent Kant on his long labors upon the critique of reason.

At last that stone in his path was out of the way, and the *Critique of Pure Reason* was published in 1781. Then, as Kant wrote Herz, he intended to proceed "to the thing of main concern where I have been wanting to make a change." [8] This change had to do with the "foundation" of his "practical" philosophy, and a beginning was made in his *Foundation of the Metaphysics of Morals* which came out in 1785.

Let us first see what the path looked like after the "critical" solution was achieved. Kant had studied man's knowledge of nature from a revolutionary standpoint—doubtless one of those new points of view which he gained in the quiet, unstrained mood of reflection of which he told. Instead of supposing that the human understanding simply gleans the laws of nature from the facts of experience, he proposed the novel hypothesis that whatever facts we are able to understand are knowable only in so far as they conform to theoretical conceptions which the mind of man prescribes as a priori conditions of knowledge. Reason lays down the logical law under which anything given through the senses is known in any intelligible relationship. Reason is thus legislative for all experience whatsoever. And our knowledge of nature is always expressed in terms of necessary and universal laws precisely because reason thus prescribes the forms of lawful order. This is how Kant explains the fact that we have genuine and certain knowledge in science.

[8] Cassirer, IX, 197.

But how has the "scandal of reason" been removed? The internal conflict of reason with itself, in those antinomies of metaphysics, can now be explained as due to men's having previously ignored the other indispensable conditions under which reason achieves any such certainty of scientific knowledge. Reason can function properly only when it legislates for data given through sense intuition, data which it construes in accordance with its a priori logical categories. Take away the given data or appearances, and thought beats the empty air—and the older metaphysics was such vain speculation. Thought purely on its own, without application to the materials of sense, runs into its internal contradictions and dialectics. But when employed upon the phenomena of experience it gains real and substantial knowledge.

Now transfer the principle of this solution to the case of practical reason where the human will is concerned. The behavior of man is prompted by many different natural drives. Just as man is equipped with senses for information about his world and himself, so he is equipped with native springs of action. As reason by its fundamental law-giving constructs a true science of nature out of the available information, so reason fashions a moral life out of activities motivated by natural impulses, desires, inclinations, and self-interest. Reason lays down the law of human conduct in the second case exactly as it lays down the law for experience and natural knowledge in the first case.

But the phenomenon of human morality, though analogous, is also remarkably different from that of human knowledge. In order to discover the spontaneity of reason and its function in laying down law to all experience, the philosopher Kant had to spend those long years of analysis. There is a suggestion in the phenomenon of knowledge of an ultimate freedom of man which seems hidden, however, deep within the recesses of the mind. Not so in the case of moral will. Here every man is aware within himself of the inner prescription of the law which he knows he ought to obey. The categorical imperative is directly experienced. It comes from within and is not a command from without. The moral law of duty which binds a man is the veritable law of his own will. And this whole complex affair, man's free self-rule yet rule by the principle of law universal, Kant summed up in the phrase, "the autonomy of the will."

This moral autonomy is reason's great role and there is something quite sublime about it. How different an aspect reason now wears—no more of that "scandal" of reason with the internal opposition of its own laws. For in morality there is but one universal and rational law and man does not contradict himself. This moral function of reason in human life exonerates reason from the charge of scandal. Autonomy has displaced antinomy, and therewith one's full confidence in the authority of reason is restored.

The new foundation of morals then is the autonomy of the will. On this foundation Kant elaborated his entire philosophy of human existence. Let us follow Kant a while then as he opens out the meaning and significance of autonomy. We can stick to fairly simple language, for Kant was here writing for the common man, despite the special terms he occasionally employed. "Autonomy" distinguishes man from all other beings. While all things are subject to external laws of nature, man prescribes the law that he is duty-bound to obey. He can appreciate this distinction within himself, between merely conforming to law and acting out of respect for law. Usually he goes along with his natural inclinations and follows his desire for happiness, but on occasions he freely determines himself to action by the idea of a universal law quite disregarding his own natural desire. Now this remarkable character of man as a free and moral being is so much a part of the common experience of mankind that the various languages contain distinctive words to designate it. Thus we speak of man as a "person" and not merely a thing, and further we say that a person is a being who has "worth," whereas things can have only value, that is, value *for* man who is an end in himself.

The dignity of man, that intrinsic worth, like Esau's birthright, is not negotiable for any mess of pottage. You cannot barter it or set a price upon it, for it is priceless, beyond valuation. It is the touchstone of value and makes all value possible—it is something absolutely basic and ultimate and supreme. This difference between value and worth Kant expresses in another formula of the categorical imperative: "So act as to treat humanity whether in thine own person or in that of any other in every case as an end withal, never merely as a means." Morally speaking, all persons are ends in themselves; they are free, autonomous persons. But a whole scene then opens up of a moral community where men are conceived to exist together as autonomous, free, self-ruling individuals who will the common law they all obey. Kant called such a moral order a "kingdom of ends." It is the ideal pattern of a whole society of free and autonomous persons.

Ideal pattern, we have said—of course it is, but how does any of this apply to men as they are? How practical, in our common-sense use of that term, is this ethical philosophy?

Kant made many applications of this philosophy of freedom in his university lectures and in several books. These we are not concerned with here. Our interest is in Kant's actual application of his philosophy in the circumstances of his day. It was the year 1789. All Europe was excited by the French Revolution. The catchwords "liberty, equality, fraternity" were flashed throughout the world, and they caught the imaginations of philosophers and poets alike.

Was Kant unmoved by these events? Let no one think for a moment that he was always poring over his barrel of notes, not aware of the world around him. His former pupils knew his contemporary interests and kept him well informed. Here, for instance, is part of a long letter from a German physician, Jackmann, then resident in England but who had recently paid a visit to France:

> The chief purpose of my journey to Paris was to be there on the ground at that critical moment of history. So I was witness to the great national holiday of the French and I was all eyes and ears

for the remarkable things that happened during my stay there. In the beginning I might have thought myself in the land of the blessed. Everyone, even the meanest soul, seemed, in his demeanor as well as his words, to demonstrate how happy he felt at living in a land where man had completely shaken off the yoke and oppression of the great and where freedom and the universal rights of man were held in the highest honor and respect. For a number of days before and after the holiday period I saw in Paris such genuine examples of patriotism and love of equality as one would never have dared to dream of. This spirit seemed, however, only to prevail as long as the people were amused with merrymaking, dancing and feasting and every manner of entertainment. As soon as these amusements ended and the deputies had retired to the provinces I heard on every hand loud voicings of complaint and dissatisfaction, even among those who considered themselves true friends of the revolution. A great many of the bourgeois as well as the noble families —and both were patriotic minded—soon began to vent their grievances among themselves to the effect that the National Assembly was going too far in its decrees and innovations, that it was much too early to stop certain abuses by absolute laws which, considering the present constitution of the state, would be futile anyhow and which sheer time alone would make completely invalid and senseless. And the frightfully great reduction of wages and salaries, almost wicked in its sheer injustice, caused very loud murmuring against the regime, and lively dissatisfaction. And it can scarcely be otherwise, since there is almost no family in all France that has not directly or indirectly had losses because a son or other relative was involved, so that the family income was diminished by more than

> half, and it takes more philosophy and patriotism than can be expected of people to make such great personal sacrifices for the universal good. On the other hand, the mob knows no limits to its own demands and claims, feeling now its influence and power and abusing both, perhaps to its own destruction. Instead of keeping guard over the noble jewel of freedom which it now possesses, lawful freedom, they run on in unrestrained lawlessness; they no longer obey the laws but take everything into their own hands and make perfectly arbitrary decisions, and every day I saw examples of this in Paris. It is the mob and a few agitators that rule all France at this moment. I have been in the National Assembly many times when it was compelled to promulgate certain decrees and when no one dared to present the least objection thereto without the risk of being insulted by the mob in the public gallery who would yell out against him as an aristocrat. . . . What the final outcome of all this will be no one can predict with any show of probability. Those who take the most optimistic view of the matter believe that France will have to suffer many another change before its constitution will be firmly established. Others, who perhaps see everything in its darkest aspect, fear that national bankruptcy is unavoidable and that a civil war is the necessary consequence. . . . The fate of their country is the chief subject of conversation today of the people of France.[9]

What was Kant's own personal attitude toward this event and its long-drawn-out sequel? Here was a new democracy crying liberty, equality, fraternity, yet in truth freedom was being quite dishonored. Such rule of the mob was against all law, order, peace, and equal

[9] Cassirer, X, 47-49.

liberty itself. The revolutionaries were deserting the very moral principle which had given their cause its initial appeal and momentum. They were following demagogic leaders and orators, and they governed by arbitrary decree. Armies were soon to threaten the peace of the continent, since the revolution could not be contained within France. A series of wars against resisting coalitions was to come—this in Europe at large. In remote Königsberg, Kant himself very soon felt the effect of the war mentality. He had offered a small writing on religion for publication, and the Berlin censor refused to pass it. He proceeded then to start writing the revealing political essays of which I shall be speaking shortly. In his personal letters he expressed great concern, and a hope that war preparations would soon be ended, for already, as he said, "our much-prized freedom of thought has gone." [10]

In the face of the history of those years it seemed absurd to believe any longer in the revolutionary principles of freedom and equality. But Kant had faith. He was not shaken by the terror, as many were, nor was he egotistically excited by the experience of personal censorship. He retained his composure. Indeed, none of this was unexpected to him for he was quite prepared by his own philosophy for this testing of his faith. He understood the nature of the Ideal.

Two years at least before the French Revolution Kant had been thinking about the problem of the practical realization of human freedom in society. When he was revising his first *Critique* for its second edition in 1787, he introduced what was then on his

[10] *Ibid.,* 257.

mind in the last part of his argument where he was developing the notion of the "transcendental idea of Reason." He meant by this an idea to which no actual phenomenon of experience has ever been completely adequate and yet one to which every such phenomenon must in a sense be related as to a norm. The example Kant took to make his notion concrete was the "Idea" of a Republic. He was very emphatic in rejecting the stock criticism that Plato's republic is merely utopian or visionary. The validity of it, he maintained, could be demonstrated in a modern form. The Republic is the ideal

> constitution allowing the greatest possible human freedom in accordance with laws by which the freedom of each is made to be consistent with that of all the others. . . . This is a *necessary idea* which has to be taken as fundamental, not only for the first formation of the constitution but for all its laws thereafter. . . . This perfect state may indeed never come into being; nonetheless, that fact does not invalidate the rightness of the idea which holds up this maxim as the archetype toward which the actual system of law and order for mankind may advance as a goal. For what is to be the highest stage, where mankind may have to come to a halt, and how great a gulf may ever have to be left between the idea and its realization, these are questions which no one can or ought to answer. For the event depends upon freedom; and it is in the power of freedom to pass beyond any and every specified limit.[11]

"The event depends upon freedom." And who shall pronounce the limits of man's possible realiza-

[11] *Critique of Pure Reason,* B373-374.

tion of such freedom and of a society having the form of a republic?

The year of publication of that second edition of the *Critique of Pure Reason* was 1787, and it happened to be the very year of the meeting of the Constitutional Convention in Philadelphia, "to form a more perfect union" and to secure the blessings of liberty through a new constitution for the American republic. In reminding ourselves of that coincidence I do not mean to claim that there was any actual historical connection between the foundation of the American constitutional republic and Kant's philosophy of politics. Kant himself would not have thought, anyhow, of deriving his principles from study of the American experience. Fundamental principles, according to him, are not to be derived from experience—on the contrary, it is only by reference to them that men can judge the state of the nation and its need of a new constitution. The principles constitute the norm of a perfect commonwealth and they lead the way. Neither success nor failure, be it in 1787 or in 1789, could alter the constructive validity of the Idea which had its own foundation in reason.[12]

[12] Notwithstanding my disclaimer here to be showing any historical connection I find it striking nonetheless that Hume's previously published essay, "The Idea of a Perfect Commonwealth," which seems to have been studied by the American founders, actually justified an inquiry into the Ideal in the following words: "Why may we not inquire what is the most perfect of all, though the common botched and inaccurate governments seem to serve the purposes of society. . . . And who knows . . . but, in some future age, an opportunity might be afforded of reducing the theory to practice either by a dissolution of some old government or by the combination of men

Now certain philosophers in Germany had utterly failed to appreciate Kant's point about the transcendental idea doing practical work in the world, and they even poked fun at his position and cited the popular adage: "That may be all right in theory but it doesn't do in practice." This provoked Kant into writing three essays for the "Berlin Monthly Magazine" to show the fallacy of the notion that theory is not necessary for practice. No one, he said, can claim to be very well versed or knowledgeable in a practical way who has contempt for theory. He simply discloses that he is an ignoramus in his line of work when he supposes that by blindly feeling around in all sorts of experiments he can get farther ahead than a theory will bring him. It is first necessary to assemble certain *principles,* for these are what actually constitute theory. And above all, one must have *thought about the whole matter* which, when one proceeds about it in a methodical manner, is called system.[13]

After this declaration concerning proper philosophical method Kant discussed his thesis in three sections: the first on the value of moral theory in general, the second on that of political theory, and the third on that of a theory of international relations. The essays were intended to vindicate Kant's moral philosophy as a whole—as being, in the proper sense of the term, "practical."

---

to form a new one in some distant part of the world? In all cases it must be advantageous to know what is the most perfect in the kind, *that we may be able to bring any real constitution or form of government as near it as possible . . . ." David Hume's Political Essays, op. cit.,* pp. 145 f. Italics mine.

[13] Cassirer, VI, 358. Italics mine.

Indeed, it is worth noting in passing that Kant repeats here the very expression which he had used in connection with the original predicament of reason, that "scandal" from which the *Critique of Pure Reason* had to exculpate reason. It would, he says in this later work, be a "scandal of philosophy" if what is right in idea were really without any value for practice.[14] And shortly afterward, in the preliminary articles of the *Essay on Perpetual Peace,* he remarks that it is a "scandal," too, that any state should be under the domination of another state, this being the scandal of unfreedom.[15] So the cause of freedom and that of practical reason were once again one and the same. As before, this is a philosophy of freedom as much as it is a philosophy in justification of reason. A whole set of moral conceptions is at stake in Kant's answer to the challenge of those who had disbelieved in the value of his moral philosophy: the equal freedom of men; the moral autonomy of each man as a person; the community or "kingdom" where each one is an end in himself; the common law, self-legislated and universal and binding everyone equally, without privileges or disabilities; and, comprehending all these concepts, the "idea of reason," the Republic as the ideal system in which all these things are possible and toward which men can move by their own will and reason. It was action also Kant had in mind. "Our times," he dryly remarked, "are so full of talk and so empty in deeds." [16]

[14] *Ibid.,* p. 359.
[15] *Ibid.,* p. 430.
[16] *Ibid.,* p. 359.

Discussing in his second essay *Of Theory and Practice* the conditions of human life in the "civil union," the state, Kant insisted as strongly as Hobbes had ever done that a civil state is only possible on condition that the laws have force behind them. But how then can man be free at all in such political society? The answer is given in the same language which we have quoted from the last part of the *Critique of Pure Reason*. It reads now: law is the necessary limitation of the freedom of each one to the condition that it shall be in agreement with the freedom of everyone else in so far as this is feasible according to universal law, and civil law is the body of these outer laws which make such a thoroughgoing agreement possible. . . . Here is a relationship of free men . . . living under laws which have force to serve their common and shared freedom.[17] Any actual commonwealth whatsoever, imperfect though it be, must be constituted in accordance with this system of ideas. The only question is, in any particular case, how much enlightenment men actually have regarding the fundamental conditions of a genuine life in society.

Since Kant's essays were aimed at enlightening the people of his own time, he spelled out the meaning of his "theory" in several rational "principles" which had immediate practical bearing. The revolutionary spirits had been set on fire by the catchwords liberty, equality, fraternity; many others, affected by the excesses of the excitement and mob rule were turning away in disgust from the ideal of freedom. For both

[17] *Ibid.*, p. 373.

sorts of people Kant offered an enlightened interpretation of liberty, equality, and so-called fraternity. First, as to liberty, there is the individual freedom belonging to every man simply as a member of society. Second, there is an equality of every such member with every other in their common status as being all alike subject to one and the same civil law, the law which is intended to secure their personal rights as free men in their society. Third, in lieu of the vague "fraternity" there is "autonomy," or better still, the "responsibility" that accompanies the freedom of every person who is a citizen in a free society. All three of these principles must be followed in practice if the peoples of revolutionary Europe were to realize to any extent the freedom for which they clamored. Under these conditions alone could they make the most of themselves as free men and pursue their happiness in their own way and be protected in their equal rights by laws that safeguarded the common freedom.

Protected by the laws, yes, but by something much more fundamental; the responsibility which free men must have according to the third article or principle of this theory.

The term Kant used here deserves special attention: *Selbständigkeit.* It can be translated, though inadequately, "self-dependence" or "autonomy." The latter word harks back to the autonomy of man's will of the general moral theory. But there is something bare and unclothed about the term "autonomy," and Kant is talking about man as he is, going about his business in his own station in life, where he has important things to do which depend upon him. The word *Selbständigkeit* conveys the idea of man standing on his own feet, exerting his own powers, making his own decisions, and assuming personal responsibility for them. The citizen clothes himself with responsibilities and it is the exercise of such responsibilities in the society that is the highest expression of man's freedom. A society of such men working together responsibly and with self-discipline is a community in a much more real sense than one where people are talking about brotherly love at every street corner. It was understandable, then, why the progress of the revolution had been so grim and destructive, for it lacked the guiding principles of a genuine system of liberty—and the theory as Kant expounded it disclosed to all who would read the great neglected truth that freedom is possible only with personal responsibility and a recognition of one's duty or obligation in the common life.

Kant regarded those three principles as the conditions of any lasting society of men existing together in this world. Every society that endures for any time exists thanks to some degree of realization of these principles. The Idea of the Republic as a society of free men working toward the perfect form of such a system is the lodestar by which every statesman must steer the ship of state. Some do better than others. The states that live and prosper best are those where these fundamental principles of human society are understood and applied in the spirit of enlightened freedom—the freedom of man as member of the community, the equality of each one under the common law, the responsible self-governance of all the citizens.

After the publication of this essay the editor of the "Berlin Monthly" wrote to Kant:

> To speak frankly, I have been all the more pleased with your piece because it seems to lay the rumor (to me highly improbable from the first) that you were going to declare yourself very favorable to the French Revolution, which is becoming more and more disgusting every day, since the true freedom of reason and morality as well as all wise statesmanship and legislation are being most shamefully trampled underfoot. . . . Of course, cutting off heads is easier than settling accounts with a despot by means of arguments of reason and right, be he a sultan or a dictatorial mob. The French can only cut off heads, they don't submit themselves to the rigorous discipline of reason.[18]

From that letter it is clear that Kant had been suspected by some of being too "liberal." Even the editor who thought it improbable had been affected by the rumor. Later, when the *Essay on Perpetual Peace* came out, Wilhelm von Humboldt confessed that he, too, was disturbed by its "ofttimes too glaringly apparent democracy." [19] Kant had indeed made a significant distinction between the idea of a republic which he was sketching in principle and the actual democracy of the French republic. He condemned that democracy because it was unenlightened as regards the necessary conditions of liberty and also be-

[18] Cassirer, X, 223.
[19] Vorländer, VI, xl.

cause it was in fact a dangerous concentration of executive and lawmaking power in the people so that they exercised the same total power as a despot, and with the same irresponsibility. It was that absolute irresponsible power which Kant had rejected in the new democracy—but those friends were right after all, for he was, in the genuinely moral sense, democratic.

The *Theory and Practice* essays were published in 1793, the year in which the French revolutionary armies went on the offensive. The attack was made on the Netherlands, and Austrians, British, Dutch, and Hanoverian armies joined in the defense. A Rhine campaign followed in 1794. On August 13, 1795, Kant announced a work which would be ready for the press in several weeks, to be entitled *On Perpetual Peace—a Philosophical Project.* On October 4 of that same year civil war, the likelihood of which Dr. Jackmann's letter had predicted, broke out in Paris and the government of the republic was in danger, but the revolution lasted only a day. A young military genius, twenty-six years of age, had gained the limelight—Napoleon Bonaparte. What followed is known to all.

This "unholy business of war," Kant had said in his lectures on law at the university, "must be ended." We should act and do whatever is possible in this matter and not be hopeless. The "hope of better times," he wrote in *Theory and Practice,*[20] must never be abandoned. Necessity had long taught men to submit themselves to an order of law and

[20] Cassirer, VI, 394.

right and authority with the hope of more real freedom for themselves within the jurisdiction of the state. Now another universal need had come home to the nations which they must meet with the same powers of reason that they had exercised in the past. The nations must learn how to submit themselves to a union having the constitution of a republic and safeguarding freedom as well as peace. This idea was, of course, far from new. Nearly forty years before, Rousseau had published his *Project for Lasting Peace in Europe,* developing Abbé de Saint-Pierre's earlier *Project.* Before any revolution dramatized it to the world, Rousseau had portrayed with a "pen of fire" the intolerable conditions of contemporary civilization and its offense to the dignity of man. He had on various occasions given most eloquent expression to the common needs and hopes of humanity. His works had been a call for action. Kant had gone along with Rousseau in spirit. But he now brought his philosophy to bear on the question of establishing a more peaceful order by a "recurrence to fundamental principles." This was a difficult case, and almost an unprecedented situation for Kant. In the case of his other works he had made a "critique" in the sense of making a "transcendental" analysis of some established institution, so to speak. Thus Newtonian physics was acknowledged as the supreme achievement of the science of nature concerning whose certainty and validity there was general agreement. Kant had then sought to discover the underlying conceptions in terms of which the possibility of such science could be understood. Duty was likewise a *faktum,* an actuality of human life, and the critique of morality undertook to discover the conditions under which man's acknowledgment of duty is possible. Again systems of common law and even of certain rights are facts of any civil society, and Kant in effect had analyzed in that context those universal principles which make law and the social order possible. At the same time he had gone further and claimed that the idea of a republic is not only operative in some degree here and there but also normative as an ideal, an archetype toward which statesmen *should* direct their acts of government or the devising of their constitutions. Now in this present case, which was one of seeking peace among the nations, nothing was established of which one could give a critique that would disclose the fundamental principles which might then also serve as guides for a future progress. "Peace must now be instituted." [21] It is something new to be established in the world.

It was natural that in these circumstances one should proceed in accordance with previously tested principles of a genuinely social existence and propose, as had been done by Rousseau, a union analogous to the "civil union" in the state, a union by a pact for a "general society of nations." By the same token the freedom and independence of each member state and its rights could only be guaranteed if there were an "established public law accompanied by a power to which every state must submit itself." [22] On this condition, of an equal submission to common

[21] *Ibid.,* p. 433.
[22] *Ibid.,* p. 397.

law, every state has its secure autonomy in the international order. But this entails an obligation to the law which must have a sanction in case of any one state's failure to comply with it. Such universal submission and obligation, the essential conditions of both peace and freedom, had never yet been witnessed in history. For states were always motivated by national interest, and the maxims of politics remained ever Machiavellian. Facts and history seemed to exclude the possibility of nations united for peace with freedom.

Kant had confessed but a few years before that "human nature nowhere appears less attractive than in the relations of whole nations with each other." Such a remark further reveals how very complex the question of a union for peace is. It is not simply a matter of a pact between entities called states, based on self-interest. That is what does happen, of course, in the case of treaties between particular states, but these treaties are necessarily ephemeral and afford no basis for a lasting peace. A universal pact and union is quite another thing. It involves a moral motivation as well as the factor of interest, in order to give any stability to the system. And morality is essentially a phenomenon of *human* relations, and in a personal form. Any union beyond that realized, as far as it is realized, within particular states must be a union of both "*men* and states" together in a "world order." [23] Kant could see no prospect of one world-state or republic overriding the local personal relationships of men in their several nation-states, for it is there that

[23] *Ibid.*, p. 434, n. 3.

duty has its first realization in human life. All one can hope for is the *extension* of the sphere of influence of such moral obligation so that men might come to see that besides their duties within their immediate society they have a duty to humanity beyond, to make a secure peace among free, autonomous nations.

The way to peace is hard. Before one can hope to effect anything there are certain preliminary articles of agreement which must be put into practice. Old habits must first be broken. Some obvious practices of statecraft must be clearly eliminated if there is to be any success. Peace treaties, for instance, made with secret reservations are a snare and delusion—they must be recognized as such beforehand. No state should be alienated to another—it is a society of men who cannot rightly be disposed of regardless of their own will. Standing armies, too, constitute a perpetual menace, and so are war debts between states. And states have no business interfering with either the constitution or the government of others. If hostilities have to be resorted to, they should not be conducted in such a manner as to destroy all confidence in any possible peace in the future. A prior renunciation, in short, of all Machiavellianism in politics is a necessary condition of any progress.

But if this is once done, the definitive articles of a union for a durable peace can be agreed upon to good effect. They are these: The constitution of each member state must be "republican." This is essential for various reasons. Only in a republican system do men have equal and "inalienable rights." [24] A republic is also a community which values freedom above all else and where individual persons have the opportunity of being moral agents, enjoying autonomy and with it the necessary responsibility and the capacity for acting from obligation. Without that moral actuality of duty in the individual members of each nation there is little or nothing to be hoped for in the relations between whole nations. Further, a modern state organized as a republic is one which has a "representative system" [25] of government where the people at large have some way of making their voice heard in public affairs, and especially in the matter of war and peace.[26] They will make themselves heard, and they will make the voice of duty heard in the conduct of politics. For Kant insisted again and again in these writings that the "moral disposition in men," though it was only too often slumbering, could be counted upon some day to gain the ascendancy over "the evil principle" [27] in their lives and thus move nations to take the steps needful for their peace and freedom.

We have said earlier that there was no established institution in history of which Kant could make a critique as he had made critiques of scientific knowledge and of morality and of civil society in the form of the state. But that was too extreme a statement.

[24] *Ibid.,* p. 435 n.
[25] *Ibid.,* p. 438.
[26] Cf. *Ibid.,* p. 396.
[27] *Ibid.,* p. 440.

For Kant himself spoke of the existence of a particular form of republic which might become the suitable agency for progress toward a durable peace. A "federal union," he declared, can well serve as a "surrogate for a world republic." It is the form which the idea of republic might take in the present epoch of history. A "free federalism" is practical.[28]

Let us conclude with words of vision and hope from the philosopher of Königsberg in the days when Europe was in the throes of war and endless threats of future war:

> If it ever happens by good chance that some powerful and enlightened people are able to form themselves into a Republic (which by nature must be inclined toward lasting peace) then they can become the organizing center of federal union for other states which will join with that republic and thereby guarantee the freedom of all in accordance with the idea of a right of all the nations—and as more and more such relationships are established in this spirit the republic will be realized ever more widely in the world.[29]

[28] *Ibid.*, p. 442.

[29] *Ibid.*, pp. 441 f. The concepts of a "republican" constitution, of representative government, and above all of "federal union" were, of course, the leading ideas in the debates at the Constitutional Convention in Philadelphia and they had been expounded in the *Federalist* (1787-1788), years before Kant's essay. The agreement in "fundamental principles" is striking. The federal principle was, of course, not unknown to the European philosophy of politics. It had been extensively treated as a historical phenomenon by Samuel Pufendorf in his *De statu imperii Germanici*. Montesquieu, of course, was a prime source of inspiration for the designers of the United States Constitution. See his *Spirit of the Laws,* especially Book IX.

Kant admitted to a close friend that these were "reveries on peace." [30] But, as he said, "the event depends on freedom," and who shall dare draw the line or at any time abandon all hope?

In the final analysis it is the moral will that counts. "To seek peace is a duty" [31] and it is part of man's striving toward his own freedom. The moral man, when he conceives of the law that obliges him, conceives of an absolutely universal principle. He cannot think of excepting himself from the obligation; nor can he limit it to his nation. It applies to all humanity. All men are ends in themselves—every person, wherever he is, ought to be credited with the moral capacity to be free and self-governing, to be autonomous and responsible. The freedom which a moral being values, then, is freedom for all persons and all peoples. Hence the obligation to extend the idea of republic without limit.

Kant had constant faith in the moral imperative. He had a hopeful spirit. He urged men to make their moral demands for peace upon their own governments. His essay ends: "If it be a *duty* to realize a state of affairs where there is universal public law and right, and there is *some ground for hope,* be it only of an unending but progressive approach thereto, then lasting peace is no empty idea at all but a *task for us to perform.* And if we do it, gaining step by step, it comes increasingly nearer the goal, for we have reason to hope that the same degrees of progress will occur in shorter and shorter periods of time." [32]

[30] Cassirer, X, 280.
[31] Cassirer, VI, 474.
[32] *Ibid.*

Kant never saw the end of the wars of his world. He died when Napoleon was starting his career of conquest.

Reason, faith, hope, duty, law, freedom, responsibility, peace: these were the last thoughts of Kant formulated in "fundamental principles," and practical ones for his world. They are still practical for us in our present world.

SELECTED BIBLIOGRAPHY

SELECTED BIBLIOGRAPHY

The Question of Man

Buber, M. *Between Man and Man.* New York, 1948.

Cassirer, E. *Rousseau, Kant, Goethe.* Princeton, 1945.

Erdmann, B. (ed.). *Reflexionen Kants zur Anthropologie.* Leipzig, 1882.

Hartmann, N. *Ethics.* London, 1932.

Heidegger, M. *Kant und das Problem der Metaphysik.* Frankfurt, 1951.

Hoernle, R. F. A. "Kant's Concept of the Intrinsic Worth of Every Rational Being," *Personalist,* 24 (1943), 130-146.

Kroner, R. *The Primacy of Faith.* New York, 1944.

Krüger, G. *Philosophie und Moral in der Kantischen Kritik.* Tübingen, 1931.

Paton, H. H. *The Categorical Imperative.* Chicago, 1948.

Paulsen, F. *Immanuel Kant.* New York, 1910.

Taylor, A. E. *The Faith of a Moralist.* London, 1930.

Teale, A. E. *Kantian Ethics.* London, 1951.

Wallace, W. *Kant.* Edinburgh and London, 1902.

Webb, C. C. J. *Problems in the Relations of God and Man.* London, 1911.

The Philosophy of Existence

Blackham, H. J. *Six Existentialist Thinkers.* London, 1951.

Cassirer, E. *The Philosophy of Symbolic Form.* New Haven, 1953.

Hegel, G. W. F. *Phänomenologie des Geistes*. Leipzig, 1943.

———. *Logik*. Leipzig, 1948.

Heidegger, M. *Sein und Zeit*. Tübingen, 1949.

———. *Einführung in die Metaphysik*. Tübingen, 1953.

———. *Kant und das Problem der Metaphysik*. Frankfurt, 1951.

Heinemann, F. H. *Existentialism and the Modern Predicament*. New York, 1953.

Jaspers, K. *Philosophie*. Heidelberg, 1948.

———. *Reason and Anti-Reason in Our Time*. New Haven, 1952.

Kierkegaard, S. *Sickness unto Death*. Princeton, 1951.

———. *Philosophical Fragments*. Princeton, 1936.

Müller, M. *Existenzphilosophie im geistigen Leben der Gegenwart*. Heidelberg, 1949.

Von Rintelen, F. J. *Philosophie der Endlichkeit*. Meisenheim, 1951.

Aesthetics and Criticism

Basch, V. *Essai critique sur l'esthétique de Kant*. Paris, 1927.

Bäumler, A. *Kants Kritik der Urteilskraft: Ihre Geschichte und Systematik*. Halle, 1923.

Cassirer, E. *Kants Leben und Lehre*. Berlin, 1921.

Cassirer, H. W. *A Commentary on Kant's Critique of Judgment*. London, 1938.

Cohen, H. *Kants Begründung der Aesthetik*. Berlin, 1889.

Croce, B. "A proposito di un edizione italiana della 'Critica del giudizio' " (1907), reprinted in *Saggio sullo Hegel,* Bari, 1948.

Denckmann, G. *Kants Philosophie des Aesthetischen.* Heidelberg, 1947.

Macmillan, R. A. C. *The Crowning Phase of the Critical Philosophy: A Study of Kant's Critique of Judgment.* London, 1912.

Menzer, P. *Kants Aesthetik in ihrer Entwicklung.* Berlin, 1952.

Pareyson, L. *L'estetica dell'idealismo tedesco,* Vol. I: *Kant, Schiller, Fichte.* Turin, 1950.

Schlapp, O. *Kants Lehre vom Genie und die Entstehung der Kritik der Urteilskraft.* Göttingen, 1901.

Whitney, G. T. and D. F. Bowers (eds.). *The Heritage of Kant.* Princeton, 1939.

FREEDOM, DEMOCRACY, AND PEACE

Aris, R. *History of Political Thought in Germany from 1789 to 1819.* London, 1936.

Bosanquet, B. *The Philosophical Theory of the State.* London, 1920.

Cassirer, E. *The Philosophy of the Enlightenment.* Princeton, 1951.

———. *Rousseau, Kant, Goethe.* Princeton, 1945.

Friedrich, C. J. *Inevitable Peace.* Cambridge, Mass., 1948.

Gierke, Otto von. *The Development of Political Theory.* New York, 1939.

Gooch, G. P. *Germany and the French Revolution.* New York, 1927.

Hastie, W. *Kant's Principles of Politics.* Edinburgh, 1891.

———. *The Philosophy of Law.* Edinburgh, 1887.

Hendel, C. W. (ed.). *Hume's Political Essays.* New York, 1953.

Kemp Smith, N. *A Commentary on Kant's Critique of Pure Reason*. London, 1918.

———. *The Philosophy of David Hume*. London, 1941.

———. *Prolegomena to an Idealist Theory of Knowledge*. London, 1924.

Meiklejohn, D. "Kantian Formalism and Civil Liberty," *Journal of Philosophy,* 51 (Dec. 9, 1954).

Merriam, C. F., Jr. *History of the Theory of Sovereignty since Rousseau*. New York, 1900.

Paton, H. J. *The Categorical Imperative*. Oxford, 1946.

———. *The Moral Law*. Oxford, 1947.

Rousseau, J. J. *A Lasting Peace and the State of War*. New Haven, 1955.

Sacksteder, W. "Kant's Analysis of International Relations," *Journal of Philosophy,* 51 (Dec. 9, 1954).

Vaughan, C. W. *Studies in the History of Political Philosophy Before and After Rousseau*. Manchester, 1925.

Whitney, G. T. and D. F. Bowers (eds.). *The Heritage of Kant*. Princeton, 1939.